TAKING CONTROL OF SCHIZOPHRENIA

MY STORY

STEWART (ANDY) LIGHTSTONE

TAKING CONTROL OF SCHIZOPHRENIA
MY STORY

iUniverse books may be ordered through booksellers or by contacting:

iUniverse
1663 Liberty Drive
Bloomington, IN 47403
www.iuniverse.com
844-349-9409

Because of the dynamic nature of the Internet, any web addresses or links contained in this book may have changed since publication and may no longer be valid. The views expressed in this work are solely those of the author and do not necessarily reflect the views of the publisher, and the publisher hereby disclaims any responsibility for them.

Any people depicted in stock imagery provided by Getty Images are models, and such images are being used for illustrative purposes only. Certain stock imagery © Getty Images.

ISBN: 978-1-6632-2730-0 (sc)
ISBN: 978-1-6632-2731-7 (e)

Library of Congress Control Number: 2021917622

Print information available on the last page.

iUniverse rev. date: 08/17/2021

CONTENTS

PART 3

PREFACE

This book is designed to cover topics dealing with schizophrenia to explain some of the common concerns and topics that one may not think about but which may be critical to their lives. These concepts are explained to help those afflicted acknowledge they have a serious concern for their mental wellbeing.

This book has been written at an eighth- to twelfth-grade reading level to reach a majority of the readers.

Numerous people with schizophrenia also suffer from depression, mood disorders, anxiety, stress, and other secondary symptoms that complicate coping with schizophrenia. This book will help many people, including those with schizophrenia and their primary caregivers. Many readers will be able to pick out certain sections of this book that apply to their individual needs.

As you read this book, I will be taking you on a journey. So, grab your coat, grab your hat, and put on your shoes. We are about to go on a lifelong journey, written by me, *travelled by you.*

PART 1
THE BASICS

YOUR LIFE'S JOURNEY

ON YOUR LIFE'S journey, you need to be in control. By reading this book, you are showing a definite sign that you are seeking to put your life's journey in your control. You lose control when you choose self-reward over guidance and wisdom. None of us have all the wisdom we need. We need to listen and learn from others. You must begin your journey by really knowing who you are. You must follow the passion within you.

You must also listen to your inner heart. This is because we should love and enjoy our life's journey. To find the love and joy on your own journey is to search your heart. By searching your heart, you learn what your passions are and how they manifest within you. Some people are involved in many circles (of people or friends) of likeminded people. Some have only a few circles or even no circles. Those who have no circles often find their lives quiet and lonely, but can still reach their dreams.

Your life's journey may involve many people or a few. Some people come and go, although only a few of these will be significant. Cities and mid-size communities will have considerable mental-health services and more psychiatric survivors walking the streets. As they are usually on low income, these people will be wearing suitable clean and respectable but less trendy clothes. Therefore, in cities, there are two or more classifications of poor: (1) poor with their needs barely met and (2) those with a mental illness, who are poor because they do not connect with the services essential to help them.

Throughout your life's journey, there will be interactions with mixed groups of people. There are stores, entertainment facilities, and restaurants, where one will interact with various people. In larger communities, there are services and facilities that cater to low-income people. This is mainly for food, clothing, and shelter. Once again, it comes down to people's basic needs.

One finds that having one's basic needs met is not always enough. In the journey of life, there is the need for excitement, chance, and exploration of the world around you—even beyond local communities and including other countries. Thriving to go beyond one's basic needs is a part of human nature. Few people wish to remain in an enclosed territory throughout their lifetime.

Along the journey of life, one must deal with one's problems straight on and make an effort to enjoy life. What follows in this book is how to deal with the difficulties arising from schizophrenia and other mental illnesses. Enjoyment in life means different things to different people and is constantly changing. Change may be minor and hard to detect. Looking back at your life, you will see their have indeed been changes—some good, some bad, some neutral.

Your life should always go forward. Therefore, your life's journey should that propels you forward, but what if it does not? Quite often, those with schizophrenia and other mental illnesses have a rough path, strewn with tangled roots.

How does one make the best of their journey? One should observe and learn every step of the way. In times of difficulty, one must do all they can—struggle, fight, and overcome everything one comes up against. In your times of darkness and uncertainty, know firmly that "light shall shine upon you." Time spent in struggle may seem endless, but they will lead to calmer and happier times. Go through the mental health system with the full force of survival and triumph, and victory will one day be yours.

When the time comes that you gain peace of mind and have reached the early stages of victory, you now have two tasks. One is to continue your path to victory. Second is to help those who are still adrift in their illness, leading them to recovery and mental wellness while maintaining their own.

When does your journey end? The journey to victory never ends. As long as people with mental illness continue to suffer, the journey shall continue. That does not mean just you. It means all of us

Something that we all have along our journey is hope (unless you shun the hope that comes to you). For your journey, I have designed a toolkit consisting of the following:

> attitude
> faith
> knowledge
> understanding
> support

Here is how to use the toolkit.

Attitude. Your attitude shows others who you are. It shows others how you act and react to given situations, including situations beyond your control. One's attitude can be constructive, positive, aggressive, destructive, negative, or passive. The first three are far better than the last three. Someone with a constructive attitude has hope and many good friendships with other constructive people. They will likely be good in leadership roles and be able to help within the community.

Someone with a positive attitude will be generally happy and seek out other happy people for friendship. They are likely to succeed in whatever they set their hearts and minds to. People with a positive attitude try hard, are persistent, and do not give up on what they are pursuing in life.

People with an aggressive attitude hate to fail. They drive themselves hard and gain success quickly (unless they make serious mistakes in their life). This attitude is magnified in someone with a mental illness. An aggressive attitude builds strong friendships, albeit few of them. They also have good leadership abilities. They try hard and thrive for success and perfection.

People with a destructive attitude will act quickly, have low self-esteem, and have few friends and close relationships, which are often rocky and unstable. They have a chance for success, but success will likely take longer for them, and they may end up directionless in life. They typically wreck their relationships and their family life, including their personal finances. This is the way of the unwise and the foundation of a life of poverty for themselves, their households, and even their decedents.

Negative-attitude people bring darkness upon themselves and others in their daily activities (even if there are many miles between them). With a negative attitude, one finds no or little help in life. This is partly because most do not even try to find any hope or success in their lives. They may desire perfection in everything they do or intend to do but will face tremendous difficulty accomplishing their wants and needs. In group efforts, those with negative attitudes will become a stumbling block for the entire group. They spread negativity and failure to themselves and others. Their chances for success in any endeavor are slim.

A leadership role is highly unlikely when one cannot make good judgements in any given situation. This can be dangerous or even harmful to themselves and others.

For those with a passive attitude, good things may come. One can appreciate what they have. Ideal situations come around every so often, but those with a passive attitude will likely let them pass by, potentially letting even life pass them by. Often, an ideal situation will be known to the public but will not be sought out by those with a passive attitude. People will often scoff at a person with a passive attitude because they are often seem like life's losers. The only time take a leadership role is when they are put in a situation or job that no one wants, although it might seem important. Another leadership role they take on might be that of "puppet president." This is a leader that makes no real decisions and does whatever they are told. In return, the person gets to wear a fancy suit, sit behind a large desk, and enjoy the support of an adoring media and public. They have a sense of self-importance, but in the real world, they are nothing, nobodies. This situation must be avoided if one has any desire for success.

On your journey, your attitude should the following qualities:

constructive
positive
aggressive

These qualities, in the right proportions, will give you the best chance for a successful journey. You must also have *faith* and *knowledge*.

Faith. Every journey, and many new ventures, require strong faith in oneself, one's supporters, and a "higher order." Faith will guide you along your journey in equal measure with motivation and trust. You must want to have faith or at least seek faith. Faith cannot work if you put no work towards it. You must stand strong in what you have worked so hard for. Faith is ongoing. Faith requires an unwavering inner spirit that relies on strength and endurance. If you keep faith, and you will be strong within, leading to a continuous flow of faith. Strong faith will bring success in your life's journey.

Knowledge. Knowledge will be useful on your life's journey. You will indeed need knowledge of mental illness in general and *your* diagnosis in particular. Knowledge of your diagnosis will help you to be defensive and the preventive—defensive because you have to defend your body for its wellbeing and mental health and preventive because you must prevent the illness from grabbing hold of your life and destroying it. You should also be the defender of your significant others and all those who suffer with mental illnesses. You should also be a defender of the rights and wellbeing of those in the mental health system for the benefit of today's generation and those of the future. This can only be accomplished by knowledge, careful planning, and action.

Understanding yourself, your illness, your treatment, and your supports is vital for your life's journey and to help control schizophrenia. We will talk about understanding yourself later in this book. Understanding your illness and your situation is essential. The following list of affirmations will help you understand your illness and situation.

> You are normal.
> You are useful.
> You are important in society.
> You can have a full and happy life.
> You are a person.
> You have real feelings and emotions.

Those diagnosed with schizophrenia are considered to be "schizophrenics." You are not so. You are a normal person with the affliction of schizophrenia. By way of comparison, a person with the affliction of cancer is not considered to be a "canceric"; he or she is a normal person with cancer. In the acute stages of schizophrenia, one may suffer many frightening aspects of the disease. There is the potential to hear voices and experience hallucinations, fear, panic, paranoia, depression and delusions of grandeur. All of this could be summed up as *thought process disorder*.

WHAT IS THOUGHT PROCESS DISORDER?

THOUGHT PROCESS DISORDER is the bare basics of schizophrenia. To cope with schizophrenia, one must understand the basic physical and psychological factors of this affliction. The main disorder with schizophrenia is the distorted processing of thoughts.

Part of this compromised processing leads to hallucinations, both visual and auditory. The auditory manifestations can be either pleasant or harmful in nature and may even lead to destructive behaviour. Other factors that can exacerbate the symptoms of this affliction include stress, anxiety, inadequate rest, and failing to take prescribed medications.

What is happening inside the mind? Neurotransmitters in the brain are misfiring and sending signals to other receptors in the wrong order or too quickly, causing mental confusion and rushing thoughts.

The neurotransmitters try to send a signal to a neuron receptor, but the transmission becomes blocked by the chemicals in the medication. There is still thought process disorder, but it is less severe. With the action of the medication, too many neuron receptors are blocked. This causes the brain to be somewhat disabled and the person to have a psychiatric disorder. It is hoped that with newer medication, some neuron receptors will not be blocked so that there is less thought process disorder. The problem knowing which neuron receptors need to be blocked and which should not be blocked. Science will eventually lead to medications that cause fewer thought process disorders; the person will be less disabled and think more clearly, without hallucinations and without hearing voices. This will result in greater functioning.

Currently, someone with thought process disorder must learn to identify which thought process is correct and which is incorrect. Adding to difficulties, the thought processing happens so quickly that it is extremely difficult to understand the processes as they happen. Therefore, the disability is twofold: having neuron transmitters and receptors in the improper sequence and the improper right speed. Aside from hallucinations and hearing voices, this creates a severe psychiatric disability. Having the correct thought process is the primary disability. As people with thought process disorder correct the prime disability, the incidences of hallucinations and voices they experience decreases.

PERSONAL TESTIMONY

BEFORE WE TRAVEL, friends, I must first share some of my experiences. I have been involved with the mental health system extensively since my early childhood. My most intense experience was in the fall of 1981. Sometime in early October of that year, I went to the hospital for the first time for treatment. I had been seeing a counsellor for almost one year, having returned home from living in Toronto the previous five months. I had taken off to Toronto in the early summer of 1980, having given my family no advance notice. One night, I packed a few belongings and went to bed. I awoke early the next morning and wrote a brief goodbye note for family to find afterwards. I was sixteen and wanted freedom and adventure, so I hitchhiked to Toronto. By midnight that night, I found a place to stay with some friends in Toronto. Life in Toronto wasn't too bad, but after five months and communicating with my father, I decided to return home on November 11, 1980. To this day, I often wonder what life might have been like had a stayed in Toronto. The decision at the time was a coin flip. However, over a decade later, I thought that returning home was likely the better alternative.

So there I was, in early October of 1981, in the psychiatric ward of the Kingston General Hospital. This was my first time as a patient in a hospital. I cannot remember my entire stay; a number of memories were good, some of them even special. I felt like part of a large family there. At that time, visits to the psychiatric ward lasted longer than they do today. There were about forty committed patients, and most of them mingled with each other. Various relationships formed, some blossoming into friendships. I was the youngest, the majority being in their mid-20s to late 30s or early 40s and a minority being seniors. The mixture of men and women was fairly even. The majority of patients were in treatment for depression and anxiety disorders. There was quite the mixture of personalities, and compromises were required for everyone to get along. Interpersonal problems were rare, let alone major disagreements. On the few occasions when a situation got out of control, the nurses and staff would put an end to it by jabbing the offenders with a needle to tranquillize them. This was all done quite professionally.

The first few days I spent there are kind of a blur. In the first few hours, they dumped a pile of questions on me. This continued for the first few days, and it soon became very annoying. There were many questions. Too many questions asked by the nurses, doctors, and student doctors, all over a short period. For the first three or four days, I had constant headaches. Unfortunately, I suffered a few days with headaches because only the doctors could prescribe painkillers. The nurses could do nothing but reassure me they would talk to the doctor as soon as possible and suggested rest to help reduce the suffering. They had to follow protocols.

I was a model patient: meek, compliant, and quiet. I went along with any treatments they saw fit. For forty-eight to seventy-two hours things, seemed very out of whack—spiny, cloudy, confusing. During this time, I was sure I would be a patient for a long time, at least a couple of years. At first, I couldn't have cared less if I was institutionalized for life. I thought I was a complete write-off, with no hope and no future, a bona fide crazy man, fit to be tied. However, I was discharged in two months.

DEALING WITH FEAR

MANY PEOPLE WITH schizophrenia deal with fear. A true-life example of this is the following story of a young boy with a fear of thunderstorms. This story also illustrates a method of conquering such fear.

One day, there was a bad thunderstorm. A boy was left alone with his younger brother in the bedroom, sleeping. Their parents were gone for a while. The boy could not sleep with frequent clashes of thunder. The boy's home was designed so that the living room was at the front and surrounded by windows on three sides. The boy walked slowly into the room. Some of the curtains were closed. The thunder was loud and frequent. The boy walked farther into the room and opened all the curtains. He then positioned himself in the centre of the room, surrounded by three walls of windows. The storm was fierce. The boy stood there, shaking at first but eventually still and calm. The storm roared, and the thunder was ferocious. The boy stood alone, his brother sleeping, his parents away for who-knows-how long. The storm continued, loud and brilliant. As the boy stood there, his breathing slowed down; the rigidness of his body gave way to relaxation. The storm continued, and the boy insisted on staying put in the centre of the room with three walls of windows around him. The storm did not taper off for at least twenty minutes, and yet, the boy just stood there. Before the storm was over, a warm glow came upon the boy's face, then bit of a smile. For once, the boy was enjoying the storm.

The thunder continued for a short while, and eventually, the thunder, rain, and high winds ceased. There was just the grey overcast sky and a mud-soaked street in front of the boy's home.

The boy leaped for joy and exclaimed, "I did it."

The young boy of about eight or nine had finally rid himself of the fear of thunder, and since then, he enjoyed being indoors during thunder storms, watching them from in front of the living room windows. I know this story is true because that young boy who defeated his fear of thunder was me.

MEDICATION AND SIDE EFFECTS

THERE ARE SIDE effects involved with going on medication, going off medication, and adjusting medication. Although we have some decisions over the medications we are prescribed, and perhaps even our dosages, we seldom the side effects until they happen, now and in the long term.

The side effects can be very harmful. Seldom are the side effects desired. A few possible positive side effects include better sleep at night, but what if the effect is to sleep too long, like most of the day?

The worst side effect I experienced happened a few weeks after I went back home, after taking the first medication I was prescribed. It was mid-March 1982. It was about 8:00 a.m., and my brother and I were having breakfast. The room was cool, with fluorescent lighting above us. These two conditions, in combination with the medication, set off a seizure. I tried to fight it off and continued to eat my breakfast. In less than ten minutes, the seizure was so bad that I could no longer eat, sit up straight, or even remain on my chair. It took all my might to get to the bedroom and to my bed.

My mother phoned the nearest hospital to let them know we were coming. The nearest hospital was an hour and a half away. My brother continued on to school while our mother warmed up the car. It was still cold were we lived, even though it was close to springtime. I managed with difficulty to put on my winter jacket and boots. I got into the back of the car and tried to lay down with a blanket over me. The warmth of the car and the blanket made the very painful seizure a little less painful.

My mother drove the car as fast as she could while remaining at the speed limit. The trip to Kingston was tolerable, although I was still in great pain and my body was tangled up and twisted by the seizure.

After what seemed to be moderate traffic, we arrived at the hospital and entered the emergency entrance. With my mother's help, we filled in the forms and answered questions to see a doctor for treatment. This was long, difficult, and very painful. We were instructed to take a seat in the waiting room. The waiting room was cold, with florescent lighting. Of course, when these conditions were combined, my seizure intensified. Despite my best effort, it was difficult to sit or stand. I barely remember my mother bringing me a can of pop from a vending machine to comfort me during my long wait. I was there for several hours.

Eventually, we were led to a nearby examination room, where I experienced very long wait. That room too was cold, with florescent lighting. My seizure intensified. I was squirming in great pain on the floor. My mother sat nearby, totally helpless to do anything. She did remind me that the doctor would soon be here to help. I was not able to concentrate on what activities were going on during that time. I was aware that a few people came in and out of the room. I helpless on the floor, squirmed. My muscles experienced severe contractions. My neck pulled back so strongly that the back of my head seemed to touch my upper back, to the point where my neck bones nearly snapped.

Eventually, a nurse came in with a large needle. The needle was jabbed into my hip. Over the next fifteen minutes, my seizure gradually dissipated. By the time the seizure was completely gone, it was 9:30 p.m. The thirteen hours of excruciating pain and suffering is an experience I would never wish on anyone.

My neck was sore for at least the next two or three weeks. I also had limited neck movement for the next *two* years. The side effects continued to some degree for several years, some of them changing over the years. To this day, the drowsiness continues, but it is now more tolerable.

DEALING WITH SIDE EFFECTS

MEDICATIONS CAN HAVE dreadful side effects. There can be seizures; stiff, sore muscles; weight gain; vision problems; confusion, and worst of all, constant drowsiness, causing various difficulties. Why are there side effects? Using medication to target only the cause of an illness is difficult. One can compare this to firing a cannonball to hit a target the size of a pop cap. Obviously, there will be overkill—hitting the target but damaging what surrounds it. Knowing there will be side effects and knowing it is next to impossible to avoid side effects, the only strategy is to cope with them.

Here are two methods. Many people with a mental illness smoke cigarettes. There are significant drawbacks to smoking—health costs, financial costs, and costs to others due to second-hand smoke. However, smoking is known to calm the nerves, so this can be considered a positive effect. There are ingredients in tobacco that inhibit some of the neurotransmitters of the brain, similar to some antipsychotics. While it is not recommended that those with mental illnesses smoke instead of taking medication, it seems practical for a small percentage of patients.

Coffee and caffeine are commonly consumed by psychiatric survivors, both on the ward and after being discharged. It is also used as a stimulant to combat the frequent side effect of drowsiness. This remains true many years after my discharge. One of the disadvantages of coffee is the addictive nature of caffeine. Regardless, this is a modest compromise to experience at least some enjoyment in life.

REASONS TO STAY ON YOUR MEDICATION

- You will be less depressed.
- You will be happier.
- Talking will be slightly difficult and slurred, but this gradually improves and sometimes completely clears up.
- Once psychosis is stable, you will be able to learn more quickly.
- Your chances of success will improve.
- You will seldom be sick (mentally and physically).
- You will feel better about yourself.
- You will feel more confident.
- You will gain control of your affliction.
- You will have the best chance in living productive.
- You will live better among well people.

CONSIDERING GOING COLD TURKEY?

GOING COLD TURKEY is a dangerous therapy. It can cause a drastic downhill spiral, putting your life in danger. Your mind may become tormented with disturbing, rushing thoughts. You may feel strange muscle spasms, changes in blood pressure, increased heart rate, breathing problems, bad headaches, confusion, change of metabolism, and other chemical bodily changes.

Sometimes the effects of going cold turkey are subtle and can include the following:

racing thoughts
panic
mania
paranoia

agitation
nervousness
physical shaking
loss of concentration
confusion

Benefits of going cold turkey (albeit slight) may include the following:

more energy
less drowsiness

However, as your illness worsens, can some of the problems:

- need for new or stronger medication
- return to hospital
- damaged or broken personal relationships
- loss of employment
- danger to yourself
- difficulties operating a car or dangerous machinery
- lack of wise judgement
- physical exertion when performing physical tasks, resulting in harm to your hands and other body parts

All these undesirable aspects could result from going cold turkey.

LIMITATIONS AND ABILITIES

IT IS WISE for people with schizophrenia to know the extent of their limitations and abilities. This could determine if the individual can hold a full- or part-time job or be better suited remaining at home. Those not employable can still participate in enjoyable, satisfying social activities. Some of the larger cities and communities in North America and around the world have clubhouses/drop-in centres and activity centres that provide day programs for people identifying with a psychiatric disorder. These programs may include card games, outdoor activities, internet activities, and meals at little to no cost. These places also may provide day trips and other special events throughout the year.

A list of some possible limitations and abilities:

- driving a car
- attending school
- living independent
- maintaining a healthy diet
- intimacy with a romantic partner
- married life
- development of new intellectual skills
- development of new life skills
- maintenance of already gained knowledge
- home ownership/renting
- exercising at a fitness centre

WHAT TO DO WHEN ANXIOUS OR DEPRESSED

WHEN ANXIOUS, TRY any of these simple activities.

- Sing to yourself.
- Pour a cup of tea. Even if you don't drink tea, the action of doing something simple but unnecessary will place your thoughts on what to do with the cup of tea.
- Wash half the cutlery in the cutlery drawer. Then, once you have put them away, mix them all up. Now, knowing only half have been cleaned, you know all need cleaning.

Such a seemingly stupid activity will lead your mind to something more sensible. If you cannot think of something more sensible, count the dishes in your cupboards. Restack the dishes and recount them and see if you have the same number.

These and similar activities will place your mind at a lower level of anxiety. The main point is not to break away from anxiety but to reduce it to a lower level. Level by level, you will gradually achieve a calmer state of mind.

Sometimes, your mind is in a state of rush. Several thoughts will be rushing simultaneously throughout your mind. You need to slow your mind down. Try to forget one of your many racing thoughts. Doing this will require breaking away from one or more of the other thoughts rushing through your mind.

When you have not quite reached the halfway mark of the thought you were trying to forget, randomly choose another thought to forget. This activity will slow down the activity level of the mind and allow the mind rush to taper off.

Getting rid of depression can be difficult. Sometimes depression will require medication or hospitalization to stabilize the depression. In either situation, there are steps to take to lower depression, tapering it off to a state of calm. The most common mistake in a state of depression is to wish it away or to attempt ridding the depression in a single moment. What one needs to do is sort out the various thoughts that resulted the depression. Usually, depression (and deep depression) is brought about when the mind fixates on one depressing thought. It may not be completely clear what is causing the depression. For some people, it is wise to break down in tears and unload the heavy burdens upon you at the moment, which may have built up quickly and powerfully, causing the depression.

For many forms of depression, something to distract one from their mood could help. To do this, try to break away completely from what you are currently doing. Do something fun or unusual.

Having a strong drink at a bar might do the trick, but that is a very dangerous choice, as it can take control of and possibly cost your life yours (or someone else's, e.g., as a victim to drunk driving). Instead, try a chocolate milkshake, or go out to a nice dinner at a place you haven't been to for a while—if possible, with a friend. If you do not have the money for a nice dinner out, make a cup of coffee or tea and pretend that you have an exclusive seat at a first-class café. Let your imagination take you to such a place. To make the experience extra special, imagine you are at a first-class café in France or another overseas country.

Developing a personal project may ward off depression and fill in the empty time (for those who have extra time). If you don't have extra time in part of your day or week, perhaps this is part of the problem leading to depression.

To ward off depression, one should learn its possible and probable causes. A major cause of depression is loneliness. Humans are a social species and will actually become dull, lazy, lethargic, and possibly week when lonely or in a severe state of depression.

Other causes of depression include dealing with a crisis, including the following:

> loss of a spouse, friend, or pet
> dismissal from work
> damage or destruction of one's property
> sudden loss of money

Reread the section as you form your own habits to reverse depression. Do not think of these as quick-fix concepts.

DEALING WITH PARANOIA

TO REDUCE ONE'S paranoia, one must understand it. I say "reduce" because a slight degree of paranoia can be useful, and it is unlikely ever to get rid of it forever. Deal with your paranoia effectively, and then, whatever remains will not be a bother to you. To better understand your paranoia, think about a decision you had to make in the past and determine if you experienced undue fear trying to make that decision when it should have been simpler.

One step in dealing with paranoia is to believe in yourself and become self-driven. Develop the motivation to become firm and confident in your decision-making. Try this a little at a time, and then be firmer and quicker each time you are faced with a decision that should not cause paranoia.

Something else to consider: Would most people experience paranoia making the same decision? Your mind will begin to decipher when paranoia is justified and when it isn't. There is no simple cure for paranoia, just applying the proper mindset when making simple everyday decisions.

HITTING ROCK BOTTOM AND RISING AGAIN

WHEN DEALING WITH problems bringing yourself downhill, one can feel so helpless and despairing that they have the feeling of falling. At this point in your life, the fight is to keep on going and not hit *rock bottom*. To illustrate, this is my story of hitting rock bottom.

At age sixteen, I had returned home after living five months in Toronto. I had problems with my parents and the life I was living. In high school, I had a C average and was weak in math. Overall, I was an okay student. I had only a few friends, and my closest friend was our house pet, Dolly the dog. I was mixed up in the head, with an uncertain future, not knowing what I wanted in life.

I was confused with religion doubting all religions and believing that the Bible was *99 percent lies* I believed in a higher power. As for Jesus, he was a special man that lived a long time ago. He was not important to me. I was one of little faith. By 1985 I gained a faith that I personally could relate to, even if different from the general population. However, not well grounded to my faith by any measure.

My brother seemed different and distant to me. My parents were distant to me. I would write my Grandparents, but would never phone them. I would never phone anyone. For some strange (now forgotten reason) I was scared to use the phone.

I was becoming more and more depressed. There was little love in my heart for anyone. In school, my grades remained unchanged. I had no plans for the future. My life was going nowhere. I was down on family and mostly down on myself.

I was seeing a counsellor once a week. I told my counsellor that I had nothing to live for but I was definitely *not* suicidal. My religious beliefs became weird and nonsensical. I mentioned that my life was just about over. I described my feelings as being the "dying hum of a vacuum cleaner being unplugged."

My counsellor recommended that I go to hospital immediately and get the treatment I needed that she could not provide. I phoned my mother to tell her I was going to hospital in Kingston. Shortly afterwards, a staff person from the counselling centre drove me to Kingston General Hospital. I was admitted onto Connell 4, the psychiatric ward. A nurse received me at the admissions department and led me to my room. I walked in as meek as a lamb. I still remember thinking that this place was my new home and that I would stay there the rest of my life. At that point, my life had hit *rock bottom*.

BEING INSTITUTIONALIZED

AFTER BEING ADMITTED to a psychiatric facility, becoming institutionalized gets easier. I shall tell of the story of my first time being hospitalized and how I finally broke the cycle, also known as *revolving door syndrome.*

I had been admitted to a psychiatric ward thirteen times between three different hospitals over and eleven-year period. This indicates that in one fiscal year, I was hospitalized twice. My first and longest stay was in the psychiatric ward of the Kingston General Hospital, in the fall of 1981. I entered the ward guided by a nurse. I was led down a hallway. The first time down the hall, it seemed longer than it actually was. I was brought into a two-bed room. At the time, I thought, *I guess this is my new home. It will always be my home.* I had accepted the idea that I would be institutionalized for the rest of my life.

During my stay in the psych ward, I quickly found some positives, making this new lifestyle actually seem *desirable*. To name a few:

- being served good food
- dressing in street clothes, including night robes, if desired
- use of TV and stereo
- access to a small kitchenette stocked with bread, peanut butter, jam, juice, instant coffee, tea, coffee whitener, sugar, and diet sugar
- access to a refrigerator, toaster, and electric kettle
- various games, puzzles, and playing cards
- a lounge with windows facing the street on one side and Lake Ontario on the other, with four-panelled unbreakable corner windows.
- a puzzle room, a laundry room, and a few bathrooms (just for bathing)

Imagine staying in a hotel but being confined there. It was like having a new family and group of friends.

Some of the included the following:

- waiting for mealtime
- being to the ward
- lights-out time
- room checks throughout the night
- lack of smoking facilities
- boredom
- being drugged out
- missing family and friends on the outside
- missing family events

Despite all the pros and cons, after a while, life on the ward becomes the *norm*. One gets used to being there. The ward becomes more and more like your home. You start to build relationships. Eventually, you wake up and smile when you go for breakfast because there will be at least a few people you look forward to seeing. Before you know it, you have become institutionalized. Your whole world will never fully come back

One day you get discharged from hospital. You try to fit back in your previous life, but that never happens 100 percent. Your life now goes in one of two likely directions. You will either (1) fall by the wayside, or you (2) become a psychiatric survivor. I hope you make the only choice: a psychiatric survivor.

You may have repeat visits to hospital, you may lose many things, and you may have only memories of how life was before entering the mental health system—some bad, some good. However, one thing no one can ever take away from you: being a *survivor*. The only person who can take that away from you *is you*.

If you are worried about repeat visits to hospital, which will surely ruin your life, think *not*. I had thirteen admittances to psych wards from 1981 to 1992. I fought hard to be a psychiatric survivor and have experienced great success. I have earned three post-secondary diplomas, have been happily married for seven years as of this writing, live an active life, and serve my local community.

Currently, hospitalization is limited. In previous decades, they would hospitalize people for long terms. The following part is for those who have experienced hospitalization and are still coping. Here, I offer my experience so you can compare it with your own.

Those who have been hospitalized usually cannot leave the ward. There is limited space to walk around, and despite having three mealtimes a day, patients have a lot of time on their hands with severe limits on what they can do.

How does one survive hospitalization? To start, usually provide items and activities to help patients fill in time during their stay. Patients on a psychiatric ward usually have more activities to do than those on other wards. The main activity requires no activity: *rest*. Rest is encouraged both during the night and in the daytime. However, when awake, even when heavily medicated and drowsy, people crave activity. It seems to be human nature to do *something*, even when ill or in a deep depression.

Activities are actually part of the patients' recovery process. As already mentioned, I have been on psychiatric wards a number of times and in a number of hospitals. In addition, I have also been a visitor for many patients at several hospitals. These institutions have a number of things in common:

- at least one patient lounge
- at least one TV and source of music
- an old stereo or portable radio on loan by nurses at the nurses' station
- a snack counter or small kitchen for patients' use
- magazines to read and puzzles to put together
- a craft/hobby room

In this room, at least once a week, a nurse or volunteer in charge presents ideas for the patients. It is recommended to be involved with arts and crafts, as long as your doctor has permitted it. Crafts and artwork gives you a creative outlet to express what is on your mind. Sometimes, your hands will draw out thoughts in a way that you can see, hold, and examine, like some artifact revealing the nature of yourself and your illness. This is one way of creatively healing yourself, sometimes considered to be *self-therapy*. Quite often, a patient will find it difficult to understand what is going on in their mind. Arts and crafts allow you to mingle with other people. Spending time with and speaking with others can *greatly* help in the pursuit of mental wellness.

Besides arts and crafts, there are other opportunities to socialize with others on the ward. During mealtimes people interact with each other. The card game euchre has been played in all the hospitals I have visited. There were cribbage games and tournaments and a Monopoly board. There was often storytelling, accompanied by laughter and sometimes tears.

There were weekly patient meetings. The student nurses were both friendly, professional, easy to talk to, and always helpful. Many of them would definitely graduate. Some of the ones I have known have retired or have moved on and excelled in other fields. People would get together over coffee and socialize in the lounge or dining room. Some psychiatric wards have decks of cards and board games.

The following are some of the games and special events I experienced on different psychiatric wards, listed in no particular order.

Playing bridge for the first time. It turned out to be a lot of fun, and I discovered that one of the other players was the aunt of a girl I had a crush on in high school. The girl didn't like me, but I still thought it was nice to play cards with her aunt.

Playing cribbage. Playing this game made for a few interesting experiences. I played against a professional card shark who made a living gambling on this game. It was made known that I was an amateur cribbage player, so we would not gamble, just play for fun. I won one out of six games. I played a single game against another professional cribbage player (or so he claimed). He lost so badly, he ended up being "double skunked."

Playing Monopoly. A group of four of us was always playing. We agreed that a house turned sideways represented a house of prostitutes. The cost was double, and so was the rent.

Playing pranks on April Fools' Day. I was once in for part of March and all of April. On that ward was a little kitchenette, including a refrigerator, a counter with sink, an electric kettle (kept locked up by the nurses each night), and a toaster. Above were cupboards containing plastic mugs. In the early hours of April 1, I woke up and went to the kitchenette without being noticed. I had some string. I tied a bunch of mugs together by the handles, then tied the group of them to the handle of one of the cupboard doors. I placed them all on the lower shelf of the cupboard, with the cupboard door closed. I went back to my room to sleep some more until breakfast time. It turned out that a little old lady had opened the booby-trapped door. She was startled at first, then laughed and untied the mugs to make herself a coffee.

Celebrating New Year's Eve. The nurses on duty were willing to bend the rules that night by letting a small group of us to stay up past midnight, long past curfew. We agreed to be quiet, stay in the lounge, and not disturb any of the other patients. That night, shortly after 10:30 p.m., we pooled our money and ordered Chinese food. Fortunately, one of us had the privilege to leave the ward to pick up our order downstairs, at the admittance entrance. We had all the Chinese food we could eat, with substantial leftovers that we put in the refrigerator for others to enjoy the next day. We had a great time.

When one is confined to the psych ward, over time, it becomes easy and even natural to make friends with most. I no longer remember most of their names, but I formed several good friendships, despite knowing we would likely never see each other again after leaving the hospital. Still, as an early psychiatric survivor, it was nice to have known them for even a short while.

ELIMINATING DELUSIONS AND DELUSIONAL THOUGHTS

MANY PEOPLE WITH schizophrenia deal with delusions or delusional thinking, often resulting in poor life outcomes. It is critical to rid oneself of delusions and delusional thinking. It will *not* be easy, but one can start by utilizing the following list. The following are the "Ten Delusion *Rid* Principles." Say them to yourself at the beginning of each day:

- Delusions will not fulfil my dreams.
- Delusions will not bring me happiness.
- Delusions will not add any value to my life.
- Delusions will not help me help the world.
- Delusions will never make me a hero or lead to fame.
- Delusions will be ignored.
- Delusions will not advance me in status.
- Delusions will not enable me to control my life.
- Delusions will never reveal the true me.
- Delusions will never have power over me.

There is one important factor about delusions you must always follow: dwelling upon delusions gives delusions power, allowing them to become the focal point of your thinking. Therefore, never dwell upon delusions. In time, you will not have to recite the list above; your subconscious mind will do it for you.

PART 2

MAKING PROGRESS IN TAKING CONTROL OF SCHIZOPHRENIA

RETURNING FROM THE HOSPITAL TO THE COMMUNITY

YOU HAVE SPENT time in a psychiatric ward or psychiatric hospital. You are a seventeen-year-old male. You are a high school student. You have few friends and few dollars. You have barely passing grades. You have recently returned to school. You are drowsy due to your new medication. It is difficult to stay awake. Even with a full night's sleep and all the coffee you can drink, you can't manage to be awake and alert more than 50 percent of the time.

After a month or two, you are struggling to stay awake and handle schoolwork. You are coming close to your wits' end. You decide to talk to your doctor and learn more about your medication, including what the doses are, when to take them, how much to take, and what effects to expect. You try a change of medication. Quickly you begin to function better.

In the first four months, you have learned about diet, working with your doctor, and your medications and how they work. School has continued; you have not quit, and your grades have even improved.

This is the first step of reintegrating into the community, *fitting back in society*. You have taken the first steps towards taking control of your schizophrenia.

KNOWING PEOPLE'S LEVEL OF SUPPORT

IT IS CRITICAL to know the level of support you can expect from those around you. Everyone needs support. Supports keeps one going in the right direction and can be beneficial in one's life. A good source of support makes one feel good about themselves. People with healthy minds enjoy being around other people who feel good about themselves.

When people feel good about themselves, others like to be around them and with them. Social circles increase in number and become stronger when those who receive support *give* support in return. It is useful for people to give *and* receive support and to do so eagerly in life, starting from around age eight.

Support can be big or small, simple, or complex. The ideal support is midway between these measures. There are many types of support. Common ones are doctors and community caseworkers. Anyone involved in fitness or recreation can also provide support. Everyday supports can include friends, family, and casual conversation partners. Other types of support include group support, specialized support, and community services. These could be people at the library and volunteer organizations that deal with helping people in a variety of ways. There is town council and local government representatives. There are various special support groups that target one area of help. These include supports for the following

> youth
> pregnant women
> seniors
> schizophrenia patients
> people with low income
> single parents

As you journey through life, you will meet many people and have many unique life experiences. You will also make a number of "coffee and chat" buddies. Some of these experiences will be life-*changing* experiences.

Those with schizophrenia or other mental illnesses get to know the mental health system very well. The mental health system is divided by province (or state), locality, and specialized groups. These groups can require investment of time and money or require little time and money.

Psychiatric survivors are likely to be admitted at least once into a psychiatric facility. Many of them survive on low incomes, and for this reason, they have extensive need for mental-health services and low-income-family services.

Some people with schizophrenia (or other mental illnesses) will at some point achieve stability, education, and employment. Individuals will achieve different levels of success.

Each person we meet on our journey will have their own unique life experience. Some will be good, some bad. Some wealthy (or previously wealthy), some poor. Some active, some sedentary. Many intelligent, many with learning challenges. Some old, some young. Some well-mannered, some poorly mannered. Some well-dressed and clean, some offering a poor appearance and unclean. Some spiritual (whether churchgoers or not), some atheist, of religions. People with schizophrenia commonly have their own religious beliefs but will not regularly attend church or be a member of any organized religion. Some have travelled the world; others have remained within their community 98 percent of their lives. Some will have many friends, some few.

Your journey will likely be a mixture of good and bad days; difficult times, joyful times, rewarding times, times of failure, and times of challenge. As your life progresses, whatever happens, you can have a full life, impossible to compare to anyone else's. Your journey will be unique, a story fit for a novel.

Sometimes you will need a helping hand—a friend, a family member, or even a passing stranger. Part of your helping hand will be this book, provided you read it and use it. Remember, this is your journey. There will be people and resources to help you, and most importantly, you *must* help yourself.

GOING FOR YOUR DREAMS

WELL, MY FRIEND, you are now partway through your journey. However, one thing every successful journey needs is a dream. What is a dream? A dream is something special that makes one feels the ultimate high for a certain period in one's life.

Where do dreams come from? Dreams start early in life, from our childhood experiences. When a child is born, he or she immediately starts learning about the life they are living. There are many early life experiences, such as learning about one's senses and bodily functions. One adapts to one's emotions, which develop as one gets older. In the early stages of one's life, there are good emotions and negative emotions; these mould how one's personality will develop and change later in life.

It is these early emotions, experiences, and personalities that create one's life dreams. These usually start to take root between the ages of four and six. One's dream is formed, and over the next few years, that dream gradually becomes clear.

SIMPLE METHODS TO GET HAPPY (AND STAY THAT WAY)

WELL, FRIEND, LET'S just say, "It's a shame not to be happy." One *can* be happy. Here is an idea to consider. To be happy, you must *want* to be happy. Be where happy people are:

> mall
> market
> fine-dining restaurant
> dance hall
> nightclub
> recreation hall
> resort
> a favourite neighbourhood

Surrounding yourself with happy people is the best way to ensure a happy life. Try scouting around your community. If new to the community, seek available local resources. Is there a bus route near you? Take several of the bus routes throughout the community. This may take a week or two, depending on size of community and your available time. Seek places where you see happiness throughout. Avoid slums, ghettos, and rundown sections of your community.

Are you a rural person? Are you often around wilderness or low-population areas? These factors can offer an advantage. Being in a scenic atmosphere or fertile forest can make you a happy person quickly. You will be surprised at how trees, plants, and flowers can bring you great happiness, increased energy, and good health (including individuals with a mental illness).

On a nice day, look for a comfortable spot close to your home to sit down and relax. The place should be away from the main flow of people or traffic. Blank out the world around you and focus of the beauty you see. Take a firm, fixed look at the growth around you. Study it. Study the leaves, the branches, their size and brilliance, the beauty all around the trees and flowers. Take it all into your mind.

Around every living entity, including you, there is an aura of energy. This aura is not easily visible; you must look for it. Most people will simply walk past a tree. They will see the tree and nothing else. To many, a tree is just a big, tall, leafy green plant. It is so sad, and unfortunately for these people, they are often down and out, sad and depressed—and perhaps for good reason—but they not need to stay that way.

Look intently at a tree or any other form of plant life. Try to connect your mind and soul with that plant, and feel its energy. Focus on it; train your mind to see the plant as a living, healthy, beautiful entity. In time, you will notice a glow, or aura. All living things have an aura, but most people cannot see such fine aspects of life and the world around them. Feel the warmth and peacefulness of it, and connect with it mentally. Feel the beauty, the tranquillity. Do not think of time or work or family or plans or problems or anything else from your day-to-day life. Indulge yourself in the beauty all around you. Feel joy fill your body, mind, and soul. You will feel a sense of peace and happiness. You will feel joy in your heart. You may feel a sense of lightness. This is good. Feel happiness enter you. Feel energy enter you. Lose track of time, if you can. Feel good about yourself. Build the happiness you can feel within you.

Be happy. Learn to find this place regularly. Doing this even once will bring happiness into your life. The happier you are, the happier you will be. People around you will feel your aura of happiness, and they too will be happier, and then they will be happy more often.

SOURCES OF HAPPINESS

FRIENDS ARE ONE of the greatest sources of happiness. This observation can be a real eye-opener and will greatly enhance your control of schizophrenia. Friends can be helpful or hurtful. Focus on nurturing friendships that are helpful.

You develop friends early in life. Your siblings are usually your first friends. One often learns important life and social skills from one's friends. Some friends will come and go within a short period. You will meet some people in grade school; then, years later, you will have long since drifted apart. A few individuals will become your best friends.

Romantic partners can be a source of happiness. These are very special relationships. You go places together, spend time together, plan your futures together. You part for a few years for secondary education or specialized training, but you return to each other, closer than ever. Sometimes you get married. Sometimes you simply remain good friends—and that's okay.

Marriage is such a special relationship. With your spouse, there should be happiness between the two of you. Sometimes, there can be sorrow and strife between you. However, true love between spouses should provide a light in the dark.

Some examples of everyday happiness between spouses:

> snuggling up to watch TV
> a candlelit dinner (at home or out)
> a weekend retreat
> a shopping trip
> a walk around the block
> praying together
> helping each other with chores
> purchasing a first piece of living room furniture together

It's easy to overlook that happiness should start at home. My own family built our family home, and that has made our home a special place of happiness. As I sat at the end of the day during the final moments of sunlight, looking up through the brick walls of the basement (the only thing that had been constructed), I smiled at the thought: our house now had a foundation.

Few are so fortunate to have their family build their home. Particularly in urban communities, this is rare. For many, their home—be it a house or an apartment—has no personal connections. However, over the years, in any such dwelling, many happy times will be experienced. Many special memories have humble beginnings. A home may be started by a couple and then expand when children arrive. This is followed by the joyful noises of a household, the commotion of special family gatherings, of holiday celebrations. It is looking out the window to see the first snow, sitting down by the fireplace, sipping tea out in the porch, welcoming a family pet, celebrating a birthday, anniversary, or graduation, laying down new carpet, helping the children move out, gathering the entire family for a meal, or watching TV with your spouse—the list is endless.

Your education may bring you happiness. Depending on the person, this will apply to a greater or lesser extent, but it applies to everyone. Education begins early in life. It is often seen and responded to as a difficult or uneasy task. However, once "with the flow" of education, friends are made, study habits begin to form, there are after school hour activities; activities with your class mates. There are those special times too during education. There is your first "puppy love," then what seems to be true love, first party, first kiss.

As education continues, you may advance into college or university. You get focussed on a particular personal field of study. You have matured. One usually moves away from home, find oneself in a different community; you are now out on your own. You likely form a different circle of friends. You take on new responsibilities. You become responsible for paying rent, grocery shopping, shopping for clothes, doing your laundry amongst strangers, find a new doctor, do your own banking, live off a limited amount of cash flow, have longer hours of school, experience a drastically more expensive cost for your education, find time for a part time job, finding the time for a social life, and many other elements of a new life and life experiences. You may find this to be a bit scary at first, but life carries on and old times fall aside and your future develops without realizing it. It was much that way myself. Years later, life is now day to day living and it is the present matters that are important. This is a new chapter of life; a chapter that had many steps to it.

Assets. This applies differently to different people according to individual perception. Although assets can bring happiness to some people, some of the time, it is a poor rout to happiness. Often assets do not last long, and the joy of having these assets are likely short lived; therefore, do not seek happiness on assets. The same applies for financial wealth. Financial wealth can be lost easier than gained. The following illustration shows how assets and finances can lead to/or not lead to happiness.

"Self." Being yourself, you have your own "Entity." As an entity, you have control of your thoughts, actions and emotions. Through your thoughts and actions will result in your emotions. Your emotions will vary. The "Ideal" is to gain happiness. You gain happiness through yourself by being your *true* self. As your true self, happiness is possible. When not as your true self, true happiness can be lost. Happiness can be quickly gained and quickly lost. Those who actively seek and desire happiness, you can quickly gain it

Community services, mental health services, medical services, and financial services. All of these are at your use, most of the time at no charge. There is no *instant* gain of happiness. Happiness comes about by the right use of these services. This *may* have lifelong effect. By these affects you have the potential for a great degree of happiness. What degree of happiness will you have? Do the right steps, gain happiness? Do the wrong steps, loose happiness?

Clothes. Just when one good outfit is outgrown or worn out, it is nice to have them replaced with something decent and in fashion so that your wardrobe is up to date. When shopping for clothes, it can be an enjoyable outing. You can make a day of it. You could arrive at the mall in time for lunch or another nice treat.

You purchase some nice clothes and outfits that really look good on you. When your friends give you complements, you feel good inside yourself. This has a good chance to lead to happiness. This could also apply to second hand shopping.

Happiness due to the needy. When looking at the needy and street people, one may feel down. Quite often, those whom are afflicted with schizophrenia will likely be on a provincial disability plan or a federal disability pension. This group of people are the needy and possibly on the street. However, when local community services used properly, people will not end up in such dire need and on the street.

When looking at the needy, you have a *real* comparison— between those who have and those who don't. The differences between these groups may include the following:

> comfort
> prosperity
> access to proper medication and health
> higher quality/better selection of clothing

Realizing just how far above the needy you are, in itself, can lead to happiness.

Community parks. Often people think of happiness as interacting with people, places, and activities. One such place that is not often thought of but that includes all three of the above are community parks. In season, these parks are fresh and cheerful. They can also be relaxing and tranquil. They are fine places to meet people, filled with beauty. The flowers, trees, and the grounds are usually well kept. If you can, try to bring a friend to enjoy the experience together.

Community safety. Some people fear the police and other authority figures in their community. This is the reverse of what it should be. The police and other authorities are there for your safety and protection. With such safety, common street criminals and the sort can be kept under control. The community is therefore kept safe, and so are you. One should be happy that there is community safety. In modern times, it has a lot going for it. Besides modern technology, in recent years, authorities have been educated in mental illness, and their awareness has been expanded.

The healthcare system. For those who are afflicted with schizophrenia or another mental illnesses, the healthcare system can be likened to a friend. It is simply sensible to respect and appreciate the healthcare system. Someone who suffers with schizophrenia will usually, at least once, require the services of the healthcare system—in particular, the mental healthcare system. It is good to know, that in North America and other advanced countries, the mental healthcare system is readily available and improving the methods of treatment and medication every year.

Self-awareness and sexual awareness. This often starts in childhood, but it becomes more significant during puberty. There are mental, physical, and chemical changes that affect one's self-awareness and sexual awareness. This is an important aspect of your health and wellbeing. They are natural. At a young age, people become aware of their bodies, bodily functions, and ways they like to be stimulated. There is a gradual and steady transition from self-awareness and sexual awareness.

Education further explains this, and by the time people go from secondary education to post-secondary education, people will start to understand these life changes as they become more deeply involved in society and find their direction in life. There will be many emotions and feelings, into adulthood. Hurt and happiness will happen. One will often be moved by the hurt; this is perfectly natural. If hurt and struggle never arise in one's life, this would definitely *not* be normal. However, along with the hurt comes happiness and enjoyment. A healthy and well-balanced person should have more happiness and enjoyment than hurt throughout their lifetime.

Fine dining. Often, an individual with schizophrenia will be on disability assistance of some sort. The financial assistance provided will likely be limited. Therefore, dining out will likely be an occasional indulgence. The happiness this provides well be twofold. There is the anticipation of the events, followed by the enjoyment of the actual meal.

If cost is a serious issue, a fine dinner for *one* can be split between *two*. This is good for two people on a date. If you are dining alone, perhaps you can afford a three-course meal. A three-course dinner can even be going to a pizza place for takeout (a slice of pizza and a can of pop), then going to a ritzy restaurant and having a simple, inexpensive appetizer, perhaps a nacho and cheese dip platter. Then you can go to a coffee shop for coffee and a donut. There you go—a three-course dinner at a variety of locations, all for under $20. This may even be cheaper than a full-course dinner at a cheap diner. This has the potential to result in both a full stomach *and* happiness.

Travel opportunities. Travelling can provide great happiness. Travel can be costly, but here are a few tips for low-cost travel.

In many cities, there is a transit system. One can pack a light lunch and a can of pop, get on a bus, and take one or more routes to their destination. One can see many interesting parts of their community by doing so, spending a good part of the day out at low cost. If you can, get a monthly pass for public transit. This saves you money and increases the amount of fun you can have. At very little cost, one can bus over to the next community, spend the day there, have a meal, and be home before dark.

Travelling from a small community to a large urban centre (or the reverse) may be costly, but it need not be beyond your budget. Develop a travel plan and calculate the costs. Save your money at a sensible rate, and you will likely have the money you need in less than a year, perhaps in only three or four months. We will not discuss how to make such a plan, as there are too many variables to consider.

Employment opportunities. We all know that it is difficult for someone with schizophrenia to gain and maintain employment. Most of us will live on a disability support plan for our entire adult life. However, many of us will gain some sort of employment. Just knowing there *are* opportunities can make people like us happy.

When searching for a job, good-looking resumes and cover letters, successful interviews, and thoughtful follow-ups all are important. Getting a job is great. But remember: it is the *opportunity* that provides the source of happiness here. If you get the job, that's a bonus. Be sure to work hard and to do your best. Why? I know from personal experience: one of the worst experiences after being on social assistance is losing one's job. When you have gotten used to living on a good income, dropping down to the income you had on social assistance can be hard. It was for me. The hardships can last longer than it ever did before you had the job. However, *do not* fear *gaining* employment. As said before, hoping for a job can bring happiness. Also, more important and rewarding is gaining employment and maintaining the job. The thought of a better future, no matter what the gain is, can bring *great* happiness.

Having the rights and freedoms of citizens of a democratic society can be a source of happiness. Voting for your government leader means making a choice. When we have fears and sadness, we can gain access to help. This is because, as free citizens, we know that the government and the law have been designed for our use. We have to realize how to use our rights as free citizens and not to abuse our rights. This will allow us to take care of ourselves better, live in reasonable comfort, and have a reasonable chance for happiness.

The great outdoors and the sound of nature is a great potential source of happiness and relaxation. I lived for five years in a rural community. There was abundance of wildlife with its various sounds, but there was also a quietness that one cannot experience in an urban centre (such as the one I live in now). The night-time sky is another benefit of the rate outdoors. In the rural area where I lived, there were so many stars, the sky lit up brilliantly at night. There were more stars than anyone could ever count. It was a mystical, wondrous experience, to the point where it was sometimes overwhelming. To find happiness, one needs to experience quiet time. Gaze up into the sky and let your mind wonder about good times from the past. When one associates an experience with happy thoughts, you can experience that happiness again and again. This, my friend, comes at no cost to you. All it takes is a little effort, and the length of time is up to you. So, head out and experience the nature that is all around you. Enjoy and be happy

Movies, music, and other entertainment. For thousands of years, people have thrived on entertainment. In ancient times, entertainment was often musical. Since then, music has evolved into a multitude of forms. In the past thirty to forty years, movies have become the pinnacle of the entertainment world, especially in North America.

We have also discovered that people's emotions are responsive to aural and visual stimuli. Since the 1980s, audio recordings designed to promote relaxation have been used effectively in therapy. Even some wild animals respond to music. Therefore, it is a good idea to listen to your favourite music, whether it is relaxing or stimulating – whatever brings you happiness and peace of mind.

The good times, past and present, can be a source of happiness. Hang onto them. The bad times are a source of pain and sorrow, so don't hang onto them. However, for many of us, this is easier said than done. How can we do so? You must first rid yourself of the negatives and the source of all those negatives. Anything harmful and hurtful *must be eliminated.*

POSITIVE AND NEGATIVE AGGRESSION

LIVING WITH SCHIZOPHRENIA, one will experience periods of both positive and negative aggression. Some people have much more of one than the other.

Aggression is a natural part of human nature. What is the difference between positive and negative aggression? Here is the main difference:

> *Positive aggression = useful and helpful*
> *Negative aggression = destructive, not helpful to self or others*

Positive aggression makes our minds positive in general and develops the will to be productive. With positive aggression, one can more easily control schizophrenia. One's mind has great potential to be one's best tool to control schizophrenia.

Positive aggression helps us build relationships and friendships. Positive aggression strengthens us, making us feel good about ourselves and those around us.

Negative aggression destroys relationships and diminishes friendships. Negative aggression weakens oneself, even one who may be strong and fit. Weakened thusly, one *cannot* achieve their potential strength. One does not feel good or as happy as one could be, and this *will be* felt and detected by one's relations. Negative aggression can even land you in jail. Positive aggression keeps one in line and on the right course to gaining firm control over schizophrenia.

STRESS AND ANGER MANAGEMENT

TO MANAGE STRESS and anger, one first must be aware of their causes. Different people react differently to the same situations. Many with schizophrenia will react to anger triggers, lashing out at a certain person or group. This is due to thought process disorder, which affects one's judgement. A minor situation can easily blossom and anger can take control very quickly. However, that individual will often calm down just as quickly. Such problems can begin in childhood and escalate to serious situations in adolescence and early adulthood.

There are ways to manage anger and stress, although achieving significant results may take several months to years. Anger and stress usually diminish in an individual's midlife. One can hasten the process by paying attention to the thoughts that lead to anger. If you can control the anger, the stress will dissipate. Try considering what can immediately trigger anger for you. Ask yourself,

- Is this really worth being angry about?
- What real worth is gained by my anger?
- Is the stress resulting from these emotional reactions worth it?

Think before you speak (or act). Might miscommunication be causing the anger and stress? Misunderstanding each other can be very frustrating and lead to anger. Ask yourselves, is the issue even relevant, or might it be redundant? Many of the issues we have discussed are little cause for concern. Our egos might get hurt, but sometimes, giving up the argument is the easiest way to end one.

If arguments are becoming stronger and more frequent, there is likely a serious problem with communication or comprehension. This commonly leads to anger, tension, and stress. Try hard to relinquish the argument, or stop the argument and reframe the issue in a calmer manner. This may seem difficult, but over time and with experience, it should become easier. As the anger subsides, so will the stress and strife between individuals.

This brings us to our next discussion: *effective communication*.

EFFECTIVE COMMUNICATION

AS EARLIER DISCUSSED, effective communication can be an effective tool to resolve and prevent arguments, anger, and stress. However, effective communication requires knowledge and skills. Here are the ten basic principles of effective communication.

- Talk face to face but not staring into each other's eyes.
- Talk to others in an easy-to-understand manner.
- Do not speak in a harsh tone. Speak calmly.
- Maintain continuity in your discussion. Do not waver off topic or become too abstract.
- Speak intelligently, with adults and even with children. Children need to be spoken to intelligently and respectfully. One should never use "baby talk" with anyone.
- Talk to the person, not down at the person. Talking down at someone is degrading, disrespectful, and damaging to the relationship of the people involved.
- Share control of the conversation. Control of the conversation should always be 50/50 to be effective and constructive.
- Avoid sarcasm and sly remarks. Always communicate with dignity.
- Carry out all communications completely positively.

- Avoid negative communication: this destroys relationships and hampers the control of schizophrenia.
- Communicate precisely what you intend to say. There should be no confusion by anyone involved on either side of the communication.

With effective communication, those with schizophrenia will live in a less confusing world and better control their lives. Other benefits include

- less chaotic conversation
- better understanding of your condition by doctors and other health professionals
- greater ease up handling personal issues
- lighter, brighter, and happier life

KNOWING WHEN YOU NEED TO CALM DOWN, MENTALLY AND PHYSICALLY, AND METHODS TO DO SO

TYPICALLY, WITH SCHIZOPHRENIA, one will calm down with a cup of coffee and a cigarette. The caffeine causes a temporary spike in your energy. Likewise, the nicotine in cigarettes will speed up neurotransmitters, improving concentration for some. Mind you, the tar in cigarettes will gradually build up a mucky solution in your lungs. Over several years, this will place a strain on your respiratory system, making it difficult to breathe, reducing the oxygen in your blood. You will tire more easily and cause stress to your body, decreasing the efficiency of brain function. This will likely lead to a stronger addiction to cigarettes. It seems so soothing to have a coffee with the cigarette, as the two go so well together.

My friend, if this continues for a significant number of years, you will gradually become slower and sluggish. You may then need to increase your dosages or number of medications. This may increase the chance you will be readmitted to the hospital. If you cannot quit cigarettes, perhaps reducing smoking will benefit your lungs and make it easier to breathe.

Cigarettes, with or without coffee, is a tool to manage stress and calm down. However, as discussed, this habit has a high price for a slight reduction in stress.

What are some other methods to calm down?

Adjust your medications, as earlier discussed.

Enjoy a hot cup of cocoa in a quiet place, enjoying the richness and fine aroma.

An afternoon nap is beneficial if you are tired and have the opportunity to do so. If you are wide awake, taking a nap is not advisable. This can result in poor, un-recuperative sleep and possibly a nagging headache that could affect your state of wellbeing for several hours. Rest rebuilds the sharpness of your mind.

Munch on a light snack with a glass of chilled juice.

Snack on raw vegetables. This is good for your body. If trying to lose weight, celery is good diet food; it is fresh and crisp. For additional taste, try using cheese spread—a healthy and tasty combination.

Listen to soft music while lying on a comfortable couch or blanket. Read a book. Take a hot bath with bath foam and candlelight, and soak there for a while. That's a good way to sooth aching muscles.

If you are physically capable, a good walk, at whatever pace you wish, can benefit you whether you are young or old. This does not require a lot of physical strength, but it can improve your endurance. This, done regularly, throughout the entire year, is beneficial. Those of you who have breathing problems, such as asthma, will breathe easier. Your leg muscles will tone up in just a few months. Use a good sunblock and where loose clothing for protection and comfort.

Some people with a mental illness will simply vegetate in front of the TV for hours, but that has minimal benefit. On the other hand, extreme physical activity can be harmful if you have not been active for a long time. Find a compromise that works for you. If you intend to become more physically active, you may wish to talk to your doctor or consult with a coach or physical trainer. Fitness clubs can be expensive, but a professional trainer at one of these facilities can provide great insights and advice on a personal training program. Fitness is an excellent way to feel calmer. This is because there are certain chemicals in the body and brain that increase in an active person that reduce stress.

Hobbies can involve more or less activity. From crafts to sports, there is likely something out there that will satisfy your body and your mind. Having a mental illness does not inhibit you from being active. Only you can inhibit yourself from being active and accomplishing your goals.

THE DEPRESSION CYCLE AND WAYS TO PREVENT DEPRESSION

KNOW WHAT MAKES you depressed, know what makes you happy, and then compare the two. What are the differences? Discover the differences and learn from them. Where do you hang out socially? Are those places uplifting? If not, stop going there immediately. Learn to be in the right environment.

Completely eliminate whatever does not bring happiness. Never use street drugs. Even if the drugs do make you happy or feel good inside, eventually, they will lose their effect, and you will need more or something stronger, more dangerous, and more costly. If you're with the right crowd, you will not need dope and street drugs. People are what you need. With the right people, you will be happier for longer and more often. As for alcohol, you don't need it. The only fluid people need to live a healthy life healthy is *water*.

GETTING THROUGH LIFE'S STRUGGLES

LIFE DEFINITELY IS not easy, but one can make it less difficult. Struggles are always temporary, but they are always a part of life. Times of struggle can lead to growth at different points in one's life.

One must have hope and strong faith. The occasional failure can actually be a step towards success. Life's struggles often cause depression. This can seem overwhelming at times, but it is (almost) always followed by great happiness and calmness.

Everyone has resources to fight depression, and they are different for everyone. There are many ways to tap into one's inner strengths. Sources may include community, friends, family, and peers.

To overcome and manage life's struggles, try new things. Socialize and exercise. This requires the will to try. Never give up, have regular human contact, dream of the life you want, get enough sleep, and maintain your health.

Life comes with many uncertainties. However, it *is* certain that life goes on. You have to learn independence, self-education, determination, and creativity.

Through life's struggles, one will experience various emotions, such as love and hate, comfort and discomfort, and relief (a.k.a., a breath of fresh air). When you succeed at overcoming life's struggles, you become equipped to help others just as others have helped you in the past.

PITY AND HOW TO OVERCOME IT

WHAT IS PITY? Pity may include the following:

> feeling sorry for yourself
> feeling like a failure
> feeling down and depressed
> feeling singled out *and left out*
> feeling alone and unloved
> feeling that no one cares
> feeling remorse
> feeling trapped
> feeling you have no hope
> feeling you are worthless to society

How can one overcome pity? A person must look at what they have in terms of skills, abilities, and thoughts that might be overlooked. How does one know everything they have? Most people have something tangible that makes them unique, personal attributes more valuable than any amount of money. These attributes also provide more value to the world, one's country, one's community, and one's family unit that no one else can replace. We are all unique.

Look at others, and then look at yourself. Do you see the differences?

Do you see what others see? Maybe or maybe not. What one person sees in them will always be different from what others see.

How much life experience do you have? How about those around you? Life experience will vary, and parts of it will be similar among many, even those of different races and nationalities. Even with mental illness, life happens, helping each of us develop. Your weaknesses will not hold you down unless you allow them to. Having weaknesses is a part of being human, and this will be true for *all* humans.

Do you believe a personal strength can also be a weakness? Yes, my friend. Strength can be a weakness. One must put in a great deal of time, commitment, and sacrifice to be considered an athlete. Knowing this, what did that person miss out on? People often see the skills the athlete possesses, but what about the skills the athlete does *not* have? The list will be close to endless. There will always be many people living without basic needs. There will also be people with far more than they ever need.

Therefore, who should we pity, those with or those without? Everyone living has life, a fundamental and obvious fact. People expect to be pitied according to what they lack, and we all do this at some point in our lives.

Consider two individuals: a psychiatric survivor (of schizophrenia or any other mental illness) and an average middle-class office employee. Both might take medication. Both might have a special diet. Both might live humbly but have their needs met. Both might smoke despite living on a limited income. Both might have a decent place to live and have all their needs met. They may smoke. They see the sun rise and set. They experience comfort and discomfort. They have their individual problems and cope with them. Both their minds may be tormented. At times, their minds are at peace. They watch the same news on TV or read it in the newspaper. The world around them will be the same tomorrow as it is now. The two individuals will judge the world differently, according to their perceptions. However, the world is the same for one as it is for the other. Therefore, there are problems for *everyone*. There is life around the world.

People are all different from each other, each of us with our own life story. What else does each of us around the world have in common? We have all felt, "Pity me." What must *all* of us now do? We must *stop* saying, "Pity me," and as result, gain control of our lives. This is a *very* big part of controlling schizophrenia (and most other mental illnesses).

GIVE AND TAKE

GIVE AND TAKE is very important. Many people are involved in helping you:

> family
> caseworkers
> doctors and nurses
> financial assistance workers

So, my friend, give them a chance and work with them. There is assistance available for you, but it requires give and take. You have to listen to them and speak to them when one should speak to them.

It is also important to get active and do something in society. What that something is can vary wildly. Take the help that is offered and eliminate what is a waste of time and money. Move yourself forward and help others move forward too.

Desires are good. They require active participation. Stop and think when it is time to evaluate your progress and direction towards obtaining your desires.

You will deal with people throughout your life. Some people should be given something beneficial, and some people should give *you* something beneficial. This increases the chance of success and, more importantly, controlling schizophrenia.

PASSIVE OR AGGRESSIVE

IT SEEMS CLEAR we live in a world where our lives are controlled, whether or not we agree.

Those with schizophrenia and other mental illnesses are expected to be passive. While it is true, when they are first put on medication, most patients are automatically passive due to the side effects. In this situation, one will be passive even if one was aggressive prior to being medicated. The illness itself will sometimes make a person passive. A few mentally ill individuals will be *very* aggressive at their peak of their illness.

The time will eventually come when one is out of the hospital and out on their own. You may be at home, with family. You will quickly discover, at home or on your own, that you are alone. Here you are, in a situation where you must make decisions by yourself and the feelings inside you start to stir, saying, "Spread your wings and fly from the nest." This is a new awakening.

As soon as you become the slightest bit aggressive, the world seems to jump on your back. You might hear:

> You can't do that.
> That is *not* for you.
> That behaviour is not allowed.

You may reply, "Other people do [this or that], and they are even encouraged to do so. What gives?"

Aggressive times and aggressive actions will come, increasing as time goes by. It is a matter of keeping aggressive and passive in balance, keeping life and mental wellness in balance as well.

COURAGE

FOR SOME PEOPLE, it takes courage just to leave their home (or their bed, for that matter). Life takes courage. Success requires courage as a nearly constant flow of positive energy, put in motion.

Obtaining courage in life can be difficult. When we feel down and uncertain in life—perhaps in the hospital—courage seems distant and out of reach. While living life, courage is a daily necessary substance, like a meal that that people need to consume daily. It is also true that we must choose our direction and work towards what we desire.

Get going, and courage will build within you. Courage will come as a steady and regular process in your life. To get the courage you need to develop your life, you have to move forward in life and never allow yourself to get stagnant.

You may have to *regroup* and re-examine the progress of your desires, goals, activities, and wants. Often with schizophrenia, repeated hospital stays may be required. That's okay, my friend. A successful life takes hope and determination, and there is nothing wrong with that. If you are knocked down, get back up. If you can do any (or all) of the above, that is a sure sign of solid courage.

PART 3
TAKING COMPLETE CONTROL
OF SCHIZOPHRENIA

GOING OVER THE MOUNTAIN

FOR THOSE WHOSE lives are at complete rock bottom and see no life a head of them, this section is for you; please read on.

You're a wreck. You have been diagnosed as schizophrenic, you have tried different medications, have been in and out of hospital more than five times, and you managed to give up alcohol. You still smoke and find a cigarette partly to calm you down. Your thought process is not always stable. Depression hits you often. You live with your sister. You dropped out of school in grade 11. You have a valid driver's licence, but you are unable to drive. Your finances are weak, but you have no debts. You attend day hospital once a week. You know many people but have few close friends. You want to improve your life and be the best you can be.

Unfortunately, you feel deep within you that you will likely never be any better than you already are. A friend has told you that you can improve your life if you really want to. You think this issue over for a couple of months, and you fantasize about a better life for yourself.

Then your "bubble of hope" bursts, and you burst into tears. You calm down. You phone your friend, the one who previously told you to live life as best you can. You are somewhat nervous and doubt that anything could help you really. You talk a while with your friend. You discover that your friend was once a wreck and that their doctors considered them to be a write-off with very slim hope of recovery or significant wellness.

You wonder: How did your friend do it? They tell you that all you have to do is "go over the mountain."

You ask your friend, "What is going over the mountain?" How is it done? How were they able to do it?

Going over the mountain is picking yourself up, raising yourself out of the pit all the way up and over, without ever looking back and never stopping until you have gone over the top and onto the other side.

How it is done is a difficult process but well worth the effort. Survival is not guaranteed, but failing to try is a guarantee of doom and eventually death. Yes, death – slow, painful, agonizing, pitiful, and sad for those around you, watching you stay in the pit until finally you finally walk through the valley of death.

For those who are determined to go over the mountain, you must shake off the your vices that are holding you down. Whatever your vice is, destroy it, get rid of it, leave it, say good bye to it. You have to eliminate your vices to have an ideal chance to move forward in life and to be well.

What are your personal vices? They could include: any and all tobacco products, alcohol of any sort, dirty clothes, indecent clothes, *extreme* lack of grooming, using illegal street drugs, laziness, regular use of foul language, disrespect for self and/or others, wasteful spending of money, wasteful use of time, too much or too little leisure time, poor or little effort towards your work (paid or volunteer), poor or little effort and love towards your spouse and/ or children, acts of violence and/or negative aggression, too much generosity, too much greed, lust and lustful activities, misuse of pride, staying in destructive or abusive relationships, maintaining a rotten relationship due to fear of being alone, fears that restrict your quality of living, being extremely timid at the start of new relationships, obsessions of all kinds, particularly if the obsession drags your life down or is potentially dangerous to yourself or others.

You will struggle a while with your vices, but you will need determination. To build determination, think about what you could have even with just 50 percent improvement. Here is a brief description: wearing nice clothes, being attractive by smiling, smelling pleasant due to regular bathing and washing your hair, getting regular haircuts to look your best, brushing your teeth at least twice a day, with flossing once a day. (Hygiene habits that apply specifically to you may not be the same for other people.) Learning to speak clearly and *smoothly*. When you speak, do not speak flatly but with a harmonious tone in your voice (even if you would never be in a rock band). Displaying intelligence, even if you have not passed or attended post-secondary education; there is no need to be a rocket scientist.

Going out on the occasional date can be a nice experience. Having a dinner date at a modest restaurant, ordering a modest meal along with a soft drink each, with a nice dessert but no alcohol, will suffice for someone on a limited income. Someone on a disability pension due to mental illness would have a limited income. Dating is important for those who are single. These can be pleasant experiences.

you could go to night school, (even at age forty-five) to complete and graduate high school, even with no job in sight after graduation. Getting and maintaining a good education is wise. The education system today can be complex but well worth the experience. There is very little to lose by expanding one's education. The sacrifices necessary (time and effort) are trivial compared to what you get. I personally have no regrets for the education I received; it was well worth it.

Nurture a relationship with a close friend (doing little to impress the friend). It is important to be a good listener. It's important that you care for this friend sincerely. The time and money you will spend on a good friend will pay for itself in the end. Losing a close friendship (or other relationship) due to death hurts and is a sad occasion. When one can walk away from a funeral with a speck of happiness, this indicates the time with that relationship included more than just happiness but also a sense of fullness between you and the one you lost. This is rare in today's society, but it can happen. For starters, make sure there's lots of quality time, and make every moment count with that relationship. This will make the loss of that relationship a little easier to bear over the years that follow.

One need not build a city to be considered an asset to the community. Any simple act of courtesy or help will make a difference in your life and lead to a promising future. This can include helping a neighbour shovel the walkway.

Sometimes, going over the mountain requires drastic measures. You walk away from their spouse and lives in an abuse shelter for a few weeks. You remain single for a number of years. Perhaps you have a causal relationship that never leads to marriage. Perhaps you are in a good relationship that leads to marriage, with stepchildren. These become your new happy family.

It might include getting a job that you struggle with for a long time, with low pay, with a rare chance of a raise or promotion. Then, one day, your boss tells you that you're doing a great job and you are being promoted to head supervisor of the floor. By accepting this promotion, you show your boss you can accept new and challenging responsibilities. When you wish for higher and greater advancements in your job, with strong will and determination, you get what you strived for, even if it seemed so unlikely for so long before it happened. Doing well at a job is a part of doing well in life.

All of the above scenarios depict what it may take and the perseverance to move up in life (and the strong urge never to go back down). this is "going over the mountain."

BE PART OF THE REAL WORLD

QUITE OFTEN, PSYCHIATRIC survivors develop hatred towards the world. They feel scammed, taken out of the good life, and trapped as a loser in a loser world. This is their mindset. If this sounds like you, it doesn't have to be that way. You, today, right now, can be a winner—a real winner—in this big, mean old world. To do so, proclaim out loud, right now, "I am a winner." Should anyone question you, simply tell them that you are a winner. Not a winner in the lottery but a winner of what this world has made available for almost everyone. The few exceptions are those in Third World nations and those in dire situations. Otherwise, the saying applies: "Where there is life, there is hope."

One *must* know that this world owes you *nothing*. There is a saying: "In this world, you are what you make it." Would all your suffering cost the world anything? No, *the real world* is *abundant* with suffering, and that is a fact of life. Below are some basic truths.

- There is no wealth without poverty.
- There is no health without illness.
- There is no happiness without sadness.
- There is no victory without defeat.
- There is no success without failure.
- There is no respect without shame.

BECOMING/MAINTAINING ASSERTIVENESS

IT'S BEEN SAID that many people with schizophrenia have difficulty being assertive. This need not be so. How does this problem get started? There is little known about this. My observations of the last thirty years indicate a lack of assertiveness begins in early childhood.

Many young children observe a lot of negative input. Here are some of the phrases I heard up hearing:

- "You're slow."
- "Hey, dum-dum."
- "I guess I am talking to a brick wall."
- "Get with it."
- "Come on sleepy head."
- "You're only good at being a hat rack."
- "You can't …
- "You will not …
- "Let someone who knows what they're doing do it, not you. You'll never learn."
- "You're a babe in the woods."
- "No you don't, pillow puff/wall flower."

Actions speak louder than words. Those who are assertive will always get the "better side of the deal," while those who aren't rarely will.

Now I will provide some guidance to help change this so you will gain assertiveness and you, too, will get the "better side of the deal." Let me tell you, though, these changes can happen only if you truly want them to. You must not *hope* to do; you must *decide* to do. When you have firmly decided to do, then you must take immediate action. Here's how: make a list of the features in your life that are *no longer acceptable*. Write this list on the left side of a page. On the right side of the page, write down the alternatives to what you wrote on the left side of the page. These alternatives should describe the qualities you want for yourself and the lifestyle you want to live. This can be difficult to start writing down, but once you start listing them, it will become easier.

The following page provides an example. On a *separate* page, write down a simple but detailed action plan. Make sure your action plan has a clear-cut goal, including how to achieve the goal and the date you *will* complete your goal. Remember, you are trying to build your assertiveness. Therefore, do not make soft and easy goals for yourself. Your strategy should *always* include improvements. You now have an action plan. One by one, do all you possibly can to be assertive and to live your life how you want to live it. Exactly how you can do this, only you will know. Only you know who "you" are. My friend, you are the only person who can change "you."

Certain people may be able to assist you on your way to an assertive lifestyle or desired goal.

For fitness training, there are fitness instructors at health clubs (available at a variety of costs). For financial guidance, there are credit counsellors, and the major banks have financial advisors for all levels of income. For students who are weak in language or mathematics, there are tutors to help one achieve a high-school level education and those to help college or university students. For people with behavioural problems, there are social workers and life-skill specialists available in most major urban centres.

HOW TO HANDLE PROBLEMS

TO HANDLE A problem, you must first clearly understand what the problem is. Quite often, a problem cannot be resolved because it is not clearly understood. One must consider the true facts about the problem. Never try using your emotions to deal with your problems. Emotions will pull you away from logic. When you use emotions in place of logic, the problem will be more difficult to solve.

To understand the problem, you need to know the answers to the following questions:

- Am I taking this problem too personally?
- Am I trying to protect my ego from being hurt?
- What are the viewpoints of others involved in with the problem?
- Is the problem worth worrying about?
- Is the problem superficial?
- Will the problem solve itself in the near future?
- It the problem best handled one day at a time, one step at a time?

The key points are as follows:

- Do not let emotions inflate the problem
- Get all viewpoints of the problem
- Determine whether the problem is valid

PROBLEM SOLVING TIPS

- Take a time-out.
- Have a coffee.
- Be with your spouse or friends.
- Switch doing what you're doing to a different activity.
- Eat a treat.
- Talk to someone.
- Listen to others about their problems.
- Take it one step at a time.
- Calm yourself.
- Feel free to cry.
- Sit, be still, and think.
- Change your surroundings.
- Do an active activity.
- Go to a neutral place.

- Confide with a peer supporter, counsellor, or caseworker.
- Go outside.
- Go for a walk.
- Settle your thoughts.
- Write a list of your problems (start with a short list).
- Sort out in your mind what can be worked out now and what will have to wait until later.
- Take an active step towards your problems (even if it's just a small step).
- Keep regular day hours.
- Keep regular activities or take on totally different activities.
- Don't lose track of your problems.
- Work on solving your problems at a progressive and aggressive rate.
- Go to the following section: "Programming Your Mind for Wellness."

PROGRAMMING YOUR MIND FOR WELLNESS

THIS IS A method I have devised and practised myself. To program your mind is to preset your mind to function at its optimum level. Your mind controls your body. The mind can be your best tool for just about anything you desire to be or change. Making certain changes in your mind can lead to all sorts of possibilities.

A "gut feeling" is a response you feel in the pit of your stomach, but in reality, it comes from your mind. If you have ever reacted to a gut feeling, this is a good sign. It indicates you are using your mind! Making a definite, clear-cut decision indicates a well mind. Programming your mind will allow to do more and use more of your mind.

For optimum results, to prepare yourself to program your mind, your mind must be at ease. There needs to be complete absence of anxiety, as best as you can manage. Find a quiet, comfortable place, lying down or sitting down—it's up to you. In a reclining chair or in a reclined position would be my first choice, but even sitting on the floor is fine.

Next, tense and relax all your muscles briefly. Close your eyes and breathe slowly and steadily. Listen to your heartbeat and feel the rhythm become slower and gentler. Fill your body and mind with calmness. Let everything surrounding you become softened and beyond your attention.

Seek the depths of your mind. In your mind, you are going on a journey. It is a quiet and gentle journey. Now, picture in your mind that you are floating down a hallway. As you continue down this hallway, you come to your mind's control room. You reach the door to your control room. Opening the door, you step in. Within the control room are various control panels, wrapping all the way around. Just ahead of you is a chair, offering you a place to sit. Take a seat to be comfortable within easy reach of the control panel. You have now made the necessary changes pertaining to the issue you wish to resolve.

Once you have artifactually completed making the necessary changes, you are now ready to leave your control room the way you came in.

This is something you can do daily, if you wish, with whatever time and is available to you. Make sure to personalize this concept of "programming your mind" in a way that suits you best.

STOP GOING DOWNHILL, START GOING UPHILL

THE FIRST STEP to going uphill in life is wanting to go uphill. You must be determined to go through emotional, mental, and physical strain if you are ever to go uphill. One must maintain a positive life or risk going downhill, resulting in having your life destroyed. Once your life is destroyed by your bad habits or any negative mindset, it is *extremely* difficult to rebuild your life, an excruciating pain to hurdle.

How does one go downhill? The process is slow and gradual. Some indicators of going downhill include the following: lack of sleep or too much sleep, lack of proper food, lack of personal hygiene, refusal to take your medication, laziness, loafing around the house all day, being with the wrong crowd, leaving school early, going against your doctor's orders, acting against logic/or against the law.

HOW YOUR DREAMS AFFECT YOUR BIG DREAM

ALL PEOPLE DREAM. Some people do not recall dreaming, but they still dream. It is even thought that those in a comatose state may dream. Individuals in hospital due to mental illness dream. Dreaming is a natural occurrence for humans.

Dreaming is healthy. Taking this one step further, you can dream of the ultimate life or lifestyle for oneself. This is different from dreaming at night, when sleeping. The "big dream" is the dream you pursue along the path of life during your waking hours. This is usually true for people who are well. Dreaming is also one of many methods of maintaining mental wellness.

What is it to dream *big*? To dream big is to bring to life the life you would love to have. If that big dream is a healthy, positive-minded dream, then you should try to grasp hold of it with all your power. This includes your intellect, personality, physical strength, and willpower.

Write down your big dream. It can be anything, even if the dream is not likely to happen. Some people dream about winning the lottery, knowing that is unlikely to happen.

Briefly here is my big dream. I would like to transform the family house into an addiction rehabilitation camp. To do this, I would need government funding, need to obtain my Developmental Service Worker diploma and my driver's licence, build and extension onto the family house, improve the laneway, fix up the cottage as staff quarters (already on the same property), bring water to the cottage from the main well, enlarge the greenhouse, have the old chicken coop torn down, possibly build a utility shed, and groom the property.

There would be more considerations to make this big dream come to be. The purpose of this exercise is not to write out the plan to make your big dream come true, just to know what your big dream is. It may never happen or even come close. Below is an explanation of why to have a big dream.

There are you. There is the big dream. There is the long arrow extending from you and pointing towards the big dream. The key is to live *on* that arrow.

See the possible future according to your big dream. Always move forward and never backwards, and never be stagnant.

THE EFFECTS ON A PERSON'S LIFE DUE TO MAJOR TURNING POINTS

MAJOR TURNING POINTS directly affect how a person's life will turn out. People usually have at least one major turning point in life. To illustrate this, the following were the major turning points in my life.

At age sixteen, in early summer, I packed up a few belongings, two or three changes of clothes, and a bag full of food. The money I had on me was $50 and change. I wandered in the wood for several hours, always staying not too far from the road, just far enough not to be seen from the road. While trekking through the woods, I approached a rattlesnake a few metres from a deer and its young fawn. I walked past the back of a grave yard. I rode on a wooden boat across a small lake. I waited waist deep in a swamp. I had a short stay at a campsite. I wandered down a short stretch of highway, then hitchhiked a ride to Toronto.

Once I was dropped off in Toronto, I was then on a subway, followed by a bus, taking another bus to get to Etobicoke. When boarding an Etobicoke bus, the bus driver refused to accept my bus fare and instead handed me a five dollar bill. I was on the bus for a while. Eventually, I got off at end of the line.

From there, I went to check up on a friend who used to live in a high-rise apartment building. I couldn't find my friend listed there. In a short time, I was in one of my childhood neighbourhoods, at a house I had once lived about six months earlier. My father and I used to board there for a time. I reached that house and asked if I could have temporary lodging until I found more permanent arrangements. The answer was no. They did, however, offer me refreshments. I accepted, and I left.

I walked down one of the nearby main streets. A short while later, walking down the street, a car stopped across the other side.

Out stepped a man. He introduced himself as the bus driver who handed me the five-dollar bill. He was off-duty and was trying to find me to offer me a meal and a place to stay until I could obtain permanent housing. He said that by the way I looked, he knew I was a runaway teen. I told him he was right and that I was hungry. I stepped into his car, and he brought me to a nearby restaurant and bought me a steak dinner. During the meal, he welcomed me to stay at his apartment across the street, or he could drop me off at a subway stop in Toronto with money to take the subway. Leery of this man's kindness, I chose the subway. I told him I knew someone in Toronto with whom I could live. He drove me to a nearby subway stop, and I got out of his car. I thanked him very much for his generosity and said goodbye.

As I approached the subway stop stairwell, there were two older teenage girls, trying to flirt with me. I told them I wanted to put my life in order before going out with girls. I boarded the subway, transferred to another subway train, and travelled east to the Victoria subway stop.

From there, I was in familiar territory. I was at the Massey Square complex, known as Crescent Town. It was a large urban complex that took up a large area. There was a modern park-like area at one end of the complex, with a long park and trail along one side of it. There were a total of about thirteen buildings. Of them were about eight high-rises. The other buildings were twelve-plexuses. There were many essential services there: a public school, grocery store, licensed restaurant, bank, dental office, variety store, doctor, pharmacy, postal outlet, hair dresser, ice cream shop and a library. There was also a private health club with an indoor heated swimming pool.

Among these buildings lived a single mom with her eleven-year-old daughter. I knew them from before. The mother had previously told me that if I ever needed a place to stay, she would take me in. I got to the main doors of her building. The time was very close to midnight, but I buzzed her anyway. Everyone in her household was still up. She buzzed me in and was welcomed to her apartment.

At the time, she had an older man boarding there. He was pleasant, quiet, and well-spoken. It was late. The boarder turned in for the night. I was served a nice hot bowl of chicken noodle soup and a beverage. We talked for a while. The young girl went to bed while her mother and I stayed up and talked briefly, until we were tired and I was offered the couch to sleep on for the night. I was given a blanket and pillow and slept quite well that night.

Life was *very* good there. I obtained membership to the health club where I would go to swim almost every night. I attended D. A. Morrison Sr. Public School. While living in Toronto, I attended a youth counselling service, Huntley Street Youth Counselling Services. They provided counselling for the city youth. On each Wednesday night, there was a group of about seven to nine runaway youths who had moved out of their homes who gathered there for group support. This group of people were very close to each other. I have forgotten most of their names. Although we have long since parted, the bond I felt with them back in 1980 still lives strongly in my heart. I am almost in tears as I write because my heart yearns for each one of them. I can honestly say that I loved them.

During this time in Toronto, I had dinner visits with my father. At one of these dinner outings, after a lengthy discussion with my father, I decided to move back home. The decision to go back home was *narrowly* made. For a while, my mind was strongly leaning towards *staying* in Toronto. I was just about to say no to my father— that thought was strongly on my mind. I was just about to verbalize it, but in just a *split second,* I was interrupted by our waiter, who came to my side of the table and said, "Here's your pizza."

While eating my first few bites of pizza, I said yes to returning home. In that split second, I had arrived at a major turning point in my life affects my life to this very moment.

On November 11, 1980, I took the bus home. I stepped off the bus at the Sleepy Hollow Inn, late at night. I was picked up by my mother in her white Buick.

The next major turning point of my life happened less than a year after returning home in 1980. When I moved back home, I was placed in a local community counselling centre not far from the high school I attended. I would go once a week for counselling.

It mid-October 1981. I confessed to my counsellor that I felt no reason to live, and even though I was not suicidal, I felt as if I were at the end of my life, with no purpose to live. I describe my life at the time as "the dying hum of a vacuum cleaner when just unplugged."

I received a serious recommendation to check into the hospital. I fully agreed, feeling as if my life was just about over and I had nothing to lose. I was given a ride to the Kingston General Hospital and admitted to the psych ward Connell 4.

I stayed on Connell 4 for approximately two months. I came in quite meekly. I thought this place would be my new home for life—a nut in the loony bin.

The first few hours there were annoying. Nurses, doctors, and student doctors kept asking me questions. Some questions were difficult to answer. Some questions were simple enough, and I provided great detail. However, I felt that there should have been questions by the doctors to clarify my answers, as I was rather mixed up, with thoughts racing around in my mind. Most of the questions should have waited until after a night's sleep. They did part from me for a short while, long enough to have the supper that was brought into the room.

Eventually, I was put on medication. Just hours prior to being put on medication, I was brought into the office of the chief of psychiatry, escorted by a nurse. We talked briefly, then the psychiatrist told me, "Stewart, we have all sorts of magic pills. What type of magic pill would you like?"

I thought he was stupid to talk about medicine as a "magic pill," but I wanted help, so I didn't get mad at him and simply stated, "My thoughts are racing around and around. I want some *medication* to make my mind slow down."

I was soon escorted back to my room. Shortly thereafter, at medication time, I was given a pill that I had hoped would help me. Instead, I was made far worse. All the medication did was make me *extremely* drowsy. Just when I would start to feel a little bit more awake, I would be given another pill that put me instantly to sleep.

It took a lot of effort to dress and bathe, groom, and feed myself. I managed to keep myself awake long enough to play a card game with one of the other patients. Sometimes, when they had the time, I would have a game with one of the nurses. I would a few games throughout the day, watch TV, listen to music, and practise my typing with an old electric typewriter, which was on the ward for the patients' use. At other times, I would talk to the other patients. I rested for up to half the day, and I was fully asleep at bedtime.

While I was on the ward there were some strange occurrences, although I have some gaps in my memory.

One time, I found it difficult to walk down the hall. As I walked, the hallway seemed to rock back and forth, as if I were on a boat. It got so bad that I had to place my hands against the wall to keep upright.

Some of the other patients were quite strange. One young man claimed to be a mouse. Another went room to room to drink the water out of patients' flower vases. Stupidly enough, there was fresh cool water available in the small kitchenette off in the corner of that patients' lounge. Another patient slid down the laundry chute, undetected by any of the nurses.

One night, I was resting on my bed with a curtain dividing me from the next bed. The man there, in his late thirties or early forties, sat quit still and quiet, then suddenly broke down in tears. I had never before seen a grown man cry so intently and for so long. Eventually, he went to bed and slept.

It was a busy floor through the day. Occasionally during the night, a new patient would be brought in. Through it all, the majority of patients on the long-term ward became like family. We cared for each other and offered each other peer support, even though there were disparate personalities among us.

It is known that patients need a lot of rest time, but I often had a hard time believing that sleeping most of the day would make me, or anyone, well. The psychiatrist decided, after observing me for two months, that I was well enough to be discharged.

Being admitted into the psych ward changed me for life. This also gave me the passion to become a mental health activist and advocate and later a freelance writer in the subject of addition.

The next turning point in my life was in 1985. I had graduated from high school and worked on the kitchen staff at Camp Kennebec through the summer. I packed up all my belongings to relocate to Oshawa, Ontario, to attend Durham College.

I was an electronic technician in training. I lasted five months as a student before flunking out. Interestingly, I was excellent at electronic drafting and one of the few top students of that class. I met some good friends there, who gave me a stronger stance in my faith. I believed in God, prayed often, attended many prayer meetings, attended regular Bible studies, and attended the Oshawa Orthodox Synagogue. I was known there to be Jewish, though among friends, I was considered a Jewish believer in Christ.

One close friend of mine often invited me to his apartment to supper. Together, we also observed Hanukkah. To some degree, he was like a father to me. We stayed in contact with each other for a few years, losing contact shortly after he and his household moved to the United States.

Another friend that I made in Oshawa back then is still in contact with me. He now lives in Toronto. I last saw him about twelve years ago, and we still write each other about once a year; he's also on my Christmas card list.

January 2, 1986, was my perhaps biggest turning point in life. I relocated to Belleville, Ontario, to attend Loyalist College. I was a student in the two-year General Arts and Science program. During that time, I had planned to stay in Belleville for only two years, graduate from college, and then move back to Oshawa. That was not to be so. I have spent over half my life in Belleville.

I could tell you many stories about my life in Belleville, but that would not be essential for this writing, as I provide enough detail in this writing as it is. I will say that many friends came and went; some of them have passed away.

Then in 2004, I turned forty. This was also the year of the flood. For a few short years, I lived in a luxurious apartment on Benjamin Street. It was the best, largest, most expensive apartment I have ever lived in. During that time, I also developed a close friendship with my wife, Jean. Our friendship began just before I lived there, but there, our relationship became very close and significant. As my friendship with Jean grew ever stronger, I indeed had a double turning point in life the year I turned forty.

As mentioned, 2004 was the year of the flood. It was actually more of a sewer backup. The day was April 17, 2004. That morning, a friend and I attended a men's prayer breakfast meeting. It was a great time and a little tiresome towards the end of the meeting. I had returned home at 10:00 a.m. It had been raining hard all morning. I fell asleep on the couch. I slept for only a short while when I awoke to a bad odour in the room. At first, I thought I had to change the litter box *big* time. Then, it got worse. I sat up and got my slippers on. A sewer backup had occurred. I lost a lot due to the backup; many priceless items as well as things that had special memories attached to them had been lost for good. To make matters worse, my cat, Patches, and I were homeless.

THE BRILLIANCE OF YOUR MIND

YOUR MIND IS brilliant. If you think not, you are either not living or you care nothing about your life Your mind is the key tool for *your* use for gaining and maintaining mental wellness. Mental wellness is the underlying message in this book. The one best way to control schizophrenia.

Wanting to find the brilliance of your mind? I will help guide you. My saying to everyone is, "After all is said and done, it will be up to you to discover and use the brilliance of your mind."

How I learned I had a brilliant mind. In my early days of schooling, I had low grades. I failed grades one and seven. It was partly due to circumstances (beyond my control) and partly due to laziness when it came to school work. Up until I went to high school, I had a lazy mind.

I was not a lazy person. All house chores I done without hesitation. I would come home from public school every day looking forward to go home and play. My mother insisted that my homework be done first. After, I could go out and play. I would skimp through my homework in about 30 minutes (tops) and put as little effort to only get a passing grade. A lot of attention was towards playing with my friends.

Meanwhile I had the ingenuity to put together plans to get myself and my friends into mischief. It was amazing how we could put our minds together for bad deeds, but never such great effort put into my school work.

My grade five teacher suggested that I be placed in a special school for mentally handicapped children. My parents insisted (to my teacher) that I have an IQ test to determine what should be done for proper schooling.

After some delay it was arranged for the IQ test. Too many was the surprise that my IQ test indicated that I had a "high above" average IQ I remained in public school and then into high school.

In high school I gave my school work more serious effort and sure enough, half my classes had high grades. My low grades happened to be in subjects I always have been poor at; math and typing. Although I graduated from high school, I barely passed typing; I failed mathematics in grade 13, failed grade 13 English and dropped out of chemistry. I was very good in geography, computers and home economics. I loved home economics because I found it to be the most practical class in all five years or high school.

I had a lot of struggling in college. I failed electronics with an average of 23 percent. I went to a different college and done extremely well in "General Arts & Science," year two program and year three program and then the "Social Service Worker," I graduated with a "B" average. A few years later I took "Freelance Writers" by correspondence and done my best ever with a final grade average of "A" People now knew beyond a doubt that I had and continue to have a brilliant mind

If you could, take the time to write about the brilliance of your mind and testimony on how you have been able to beat the odds of being a failure; struck down with schizophrenia or other mental illness. Writing down a journal of thoughts is another way to show the brilliance of *your* mind.

SETTING GOALS FOR YOURSELF

MY FRIEND, HAVING Goals in life is very important for sound mind, sound life, and sound lifestyle. Goal setting is important for being positive, productive and higher functional. A goal helps direct one's life and guides one to a livelihood most suitable to you and will greatly help control schizophrenia.

Sometimes a goal does not work out for how one would hope for. This is useful for narrowing the path one should go along with.

Trial and error is a good method for finding what selection of goals will lead to. Eventually goals become clearer as to what goal would most likely become successful.

For those with schizophrenia (Thought Process Disorder) goals are definitely important. It also important to contemplate what goal is obtainable and how suitable, enjoyable and fulfilling.

Sometimes one will have more than one goal to be accomplished in life and through the years in the progress of one's life. It is okay to have a number of goals. I myself have set a number of goals.

I have reached a few different levels of accomplishments of my goals. Some of my life goals have been: Social Work diploma, Free Lance Writer diploma, writing books that one day will be on the market, peer support, marriage and teaching mental wellness. Of these I have obtained or in the progress of managing all of them. Some goals that ended quickly have been becoming an Electronic Technician, nursing, Officers' college. I reached some small level of accomplishment as Electronic Technician; 5 months training that came to an end. Happy I tried. At 23 percent I feel good knowing I still learned more than if I never tried. That helped lead me down the path to becoming a Social Worker.

It is also a good idea to be aware of some potential goals. These could be alternatives for when a goal does not work out how you desired. Some people with schizophrenia are often forced to change their goals or at least modify them. In later years goals could change or potential goals come to be. A few of my potential goals are: obtaining my D.S.W. diploma, working part time and learning to play a musical instrument. These could be considered secondary goals.

Some of the factors that need to be considered for goal planning are: cost, time, ability, compatibility with your life style, age, education and skills required, your geographic location, physical and mental limitations/ abilities, culture, personal week points, maturity, mobility, family needs/ size, commitments or lack of ability to commit, past attempts at your goal and demand of the business market.

OBTAINING SUCCESS

EVERYONE CAN LEAD a successful life. If your life is not successful or far from reaching success, it is likely that you are not seeking success or do not know how to seek success. Almost everyone can live a successful life. A person has to seek and find success within them. My friend, it is up to you to find your (inner) success.

Know what is blocking your success. Write a list of what you genuinely block you from success. Here below I have written two lists. One, what used to block my success. Two, what still hinders me from obtaining greater success.

Think of all you have been through in life. I know it is likely you have been through a lot of significant ordeals if you are reading this book.

I was miss-understood by my teachers and peers. They were proven wrong and their doubts swept away. I am sure that you too had people think one way about you and then one day realized, not so

LIST ONE

NOT TAKING MY school work seriously—Hanging out with the wrong friends

Wanting fun and play 24/7—Getting into mischief—No life goals—Not looking after my body properly—Not caring about the clothes I wore or my appearance

Not obeying my parents—Not obeying my teachers—Skipping school—No faith

Willingness to break the law, such as shop-lifting and vandalizing—Being careless—Spending my money foolishly—Not seriously saving money (even being poor is no excuse for not having an active savings account)—Lack of physical activities—Watching TV too often—Lack of motivation—Following and living the wrong motives.

LIST TWO

NOT ADHERING TO a good budget—Breaking the budget that I know I should follow.

Not always being responsible with my debts—Purchasing DVD's and CD's through mail order clubs—Too generous giving money to friends—Making unwise financial commitments.

Now make a list of what helps you *gain* success. As guidance, here is my list.

LIST THREE (SUCCESS LIST)

GOOD USE OF time—Being productive—Positive minded—Maintaining medications

Keeping tabs with my psychiatrist—Love my wife—Make use of my wife's wisdom

Better control of my money—Being with people each day—Caring for my body and peace of mind—Control my anger—Control dangerous thoughts—Diet daily

Faith and practice of my faith—Prayer life

Use List Three to help change List One and Two. It can be done. Only you can do so. As everyone is different, the "What, How and When" will be up to you. *Go for it.*

THE EXERCISE FOR SUCCESS

FOR THOSE WHO truly and sincerely seek success, this simple exercise will be a "booster" for success. For those who do not seek success, close this book and pass it onto a friend.

This exercise I have demonstrated in front of an audience of 40+ people. That in itself is great. Not everyone may have an audience and that is okay. Perform this exercise by yourself, repeatedly throughout the day, week, month or whatever suits your regular routines. Just as long as you make it a part of your regular routine.

Here is the physical aspect of this exercise: Perhaps by yourself, away from others and out of sound range, maybe in front of a full-length mirror, you are ready to start. Must be standing. If not already standing, **stand up** While standing, clear your mind of all your days' thoughts and agendas. Think solely of "Success." Standing firm and rigid, clear mind, focussed; now raise an arm (left or right, doesn't matter). Now with the hand of the raised arm, form a fist. Make it a tight fist. Stretch up your raised arm and fist and while doing so shout out clearly and sharply, "Reach for The Top Reach for The Top Reach for The Top" Do this repeatedly for at least 1 to 3 minutes. When performing this exercise, it is best to reach and stretch so vigorously that you have a bit of a jump off the floor. Not to need a high jump, just high enough to lift your feet off the floor.

The functional part of this exercise is most important. It is an act that normally one would never do. For anyone whom has reached success has most likely broken away from the "*common*" activities or methods throughout their daily living. Almost everyone would likely *not* gain success doing day in day out common activities. To be successful has been briefly discussed to go beyond what everyone else has done. There is the saying, "Stick your neck out." With boldness and bravery, one *will* gain success. It is just a matter of when, not if.

SETTING PRIORITIES (THE THREE LEVELS)

TO CONTROL YOUR life, you have to prioritize your daily and regular activities. The three levels of priorities are listed as: "Must do," "Perhaps," and "No way."

Everyone has various activities in their lives. To list even some of activities would be a rather long list. Here are some basic ones; employment, family time, hobby and leisure time. With all these activities there will be "time factors" or "priorities."

Must-do. Time with wife, earning money, save money, writing, paying the bills on time, improve financial stability, reading, eating, hygiene, rest, loving my wife, groceries, bus passes, non-prescription medication, clothing, regular entertainment, walking, learning, your medication, presenting yourself professionally, zero debts

Perhaps. Take the garbage out, clean house, do the dishes, the floors, phone calls, resting, casual banking, maintaining supply of postage, helping the local community, recreation centre, education.

No *way.* Watch TV all day, playing reckless sports, move, violence, abuse to my wife, abuse to other women, spend money too quickly in any given month, do evil deeds, prostitute myself, smoke, do dope, excessive drinker (of alcohol), party all day, party all night, drive drunk, drive without a licence, dress in shabby or dirty clothing, grow long hair, vandalize others' property, make a scene in public, own a pet, move out of town, over work myself, sleep longer than I choose, help beggars downtown.

BECOMING ORGANIZED

WE HAVE DISCUSSED setting priorities and setting goals for ourselves. This is part of being organized. Expanding upon has already been discussed, we will now discuss organizing the household and family activities. This includes one's day job (or night job), finances, as well as daily, weekly, monthly, and yearly schedule.

It is a good idea to have a schedule keeper, preferably with an eighteen-month calendar or two-year calendar.

Make sure there is space to write in short reminder notes. The type of reminders depends upon your needs. These can include birthdays, anniversaries, paydays, book returns, grocery days, bills to pay, when to send out mail/payments, dentist and doctor appointments, and travel dates.

Learn good habits for staying organized. You need to learn how, why, and what you can do. The worst planning habit is *not* to plan.

Before planning, there are two things you should know: (1) know yourself, and (2) know what is happening in any given day. To know yourself is to know two things (a) what you what you usually do (from the time you awake) till you go to bed and (b) what motivates you. Study and focus on what motivates you. If you have *no* motivation, it is unlikely you will ever be organized, and success, happiness, and fulfilment will be a struggle. Being organized is the key to making your life enjoyable. Fulfilling enjoyment in your life will cause you to want to be organized. This is like a repetitive loop.

GET INVOLVED

A CONTINUING STEP towards taking control of schizophrenia is getting involved in your community or district with mental health issues that could affect you and others who may be mentally ill.

What things can one do to get involved, and how? Get educated. This doesn't necessarily mean getting a degree or diploma, but you may wish to join a group of likeminded individuals to learn a specific skill or take an at-home study course that allows you to make affordable monthly payments (instead of paying a high tuition fee for college or university). In the field of study of choice, you will find others with similar interests.

Examine the community services in your area. You may find that there certain community services require volunteer workers or volunteer boards of directors. These activities usually require you only part-time throughout the month, with a one-year commitment. You could have some very meaningful duties and obligations that require considerably fewer hours than a full-time job, as well as fewer employment requirements. It is important to be involved.

Here are a few of the possible perks from this type of involvement.

- Regular meetings, with transportation and refreshments provided at no or little cost. There are sometimes annual general meeting that volunteers are rewarded with a gift.
- The chance to meet important people in the community who can open doors to potential new community projects (allowing you to get a foot in the door first).
- Short-term educational programs that reward you with a certificate.
- A combination of work and fun. (Who said education costs a fortune?)

YOUR INNER KARMA

AFTER READING THIS, you may wish to redefine "inner karma" according to your own personal description. Inner karma will help guide you to inner peace, more mind power, a calmer mind, success, happier relationships, a stronger marriage, wisdom (by associating with wiser people), direction in life, better career choices, better knowledge of the type of person you are (revealed in great detail), and better wellbeing (mental, physical, and spiritual).

Taking advantage of your inner karma will mitigate your personal weaknesses and faults. When you learn and understand your weaknesses and faults, you can better train yourself to correct your weaknesses and even turn them into strengths (or life strongholds).

Almost everyone born on earth has inner karma. An unfortunate few are born with major brain defects and disorders, greatly limiting the ability to tap into their inner karma (however, this is not certain). The good news is that the ability to have and use inner karma does is not a factor of one's intelligence. If a person has enough intelligence to function in society, even at a basic level (such as being physically or mentally challenged and living in a group home), one may still have inner karma close at hand and for their use. Inner karma is not excluded to a certain race, education level, income level, occupation, or any mental illness.

I have acquaintances who were born with physical and mental limitations; however, they have greatly made use of their inner karma. Being around these two individuals even for five minutes boosts my self-spirit and happiness. When others around you use *their* inner karma, this will, in turn, boost *your* inner karma. The human species is a very social species. Your ability to be social is in part a reflection of your ability to use inner karma and how frequently you use it.

Have you ever noticed that people with either a physical or a mental disability tend to be outwardly happy, cheerful, and worry-free? Within only a few minutes, you will know it when you are with these types of people.

One time, I volunteered at a musical fundraising concert, performing crowd-control duties. Along came a young man in a wheelchair, being wheeled around by his attendant. This person, despite severe physical and mental limitations, radiated very strong inner karma. I had never met this person before and would likely never meet him again, but I was powerfully enlightened by his inner karma. Obviously, this man's life would achieve only limited success, but for a day, his heart and spirit were aglow. What made that possible was his inner karma.

Beware that inner karma can be used for evil purposes. Examples of this include Jim Jones (of the Jonestown affair), Charles Manson, Ted Bundy, and Adolf Hitler. Despite having strong inner karma, these individuals used it for evil. They had short-lived quick successes resulting in death and destruction.

Some examples individuals who used inner karma for good purposes include Gandhi, Princess Diana, and Mother Teresa.

Both these groups of people, whether they used their inner karma for good or bad, put their full hearts into it.

How does one put their inner karma to use? First, one must understand what inner karma is. Inner karma is the force within you that attracts or repels people and things around you. This force can draw energy to you or repel it. It can reveal the inward qualities of those near you as well as those within you. The force can draw and emit strengths and weaknesses to and from you. It is the personal life energy we all have that draws the warmth or coldness of your nature and natural wellbeing to and from you. It is a part of your personal make-up and the background of your mind, spirit, and soul. It is the energy force that makes you "you." Your personality stems from your inner karma, and in part, your personality partly reflects your inner karma.

A strong inner karma will illuminate personality, adding colour. A strong inner karma will bring you many friends, happiness, and success. With a strong inner karma, any failures in life likely indicate that those interests and goals were *not meant for you*. These are your weaknesses, but they can be worked upon and strengthened if you feel they are personally or professionally important. As for me, math skills and sciences are my weak points, so I steer away from life choices that require them. If I need assistance in these areas, I use reference materials, books, and a good calculator.

My inner karma is still being investigated and "opened up." It is my inner karma that has brought many casual friends, a few close friends, and a variety of likeminded professionals into my life the past twenty-plus years. My strong points are creativity, imagination, ingenuity, drive, and determination. Due to both nature and nurture, I am a quiet person who, when with the right people, can be very talkative. Otherwise, I tend to be attentive and observant, keeping a defensive and private distance. As my inner karma is further discovered and revealed, studied and understood, I will make greater use of it and achieve greater happiness.

Your inner karma may already be active and alive in you. You may have had some awareness and understanding. Regardless, your inner karma can be opened up, discovered, and utilized for good intentions quite easily.

Meditating on the thought and existence of your inner karma will draw it out and strengthen it. By simply being aware of your inner karma, it will enlighten you to inner peace and happiness. Keep exploring your inner karma.

Your inner karma is born in you. It surfaces in your life as you allow it to do so. It is difficult to understand why your inner karma cannot be used to better your life, all life long. You will only butt heads with those in your life who oppose you in nature and karma. Normally, you are a likeable person. Rejection comes from the wrong nurturing and life experiences. A negative inner karma may become strongly developed, but this will be short-lived. Generally, negative inner karma will repel most people, but some people may be attracted to you for a brief time, but any successes you may realize will be short-lived.

Positive inner karma will flourish and bring people with great joy into your life and those involved in your life. Watch for the signs of inner karma and the stronger and more fluent you will become.

What are some signs that your inner karma radiates a "glow" in your life? Have you ever met a person who became an instant friend? Why is it that some strangers are easy to approach and talk to while others are not? Has a stranger sat down beside you on a bus or plane and you felt a compatible, warm, friendly feeling, whereas with certain others, you feel irritable and on alert? There are signals being exchanged between *everyone*. These signals signs that your inner karma is becoming active and is indicating who matches you and who does not. A person could be an upright, good, sensible person but not match your inner karma. Who is likely to match your inner karma? Those who are like you in some way, even if you don't realize it. Sometimes, people have an outward personality that they readily display to the public, and some people have a hidden personality they suppress for some reason. Often, this happens because the person is in the wrong place or social setting. Search your inner karma and draw it out of you so it is visible to those around you. Seek the inner karma of others. Do you want to be happy and successful in life? Find those with a happy and successful inner karma, and if you too have a happy and successful inner karma, happiness and success will flourish for you both. If you meet people with the wrong inner karma, avoid them. Opposites do not get along well most of the time and will drain your natural energy. Build upon your life not only by seeking success but also by being with successful people. Live life to the fullest, and your inner karma will grow stronger. The stronger your inner karma, the greater you will be able to control schizophrenia and live life to the fullest.

YOUR HEALTH

HEALTHY LIVING LEADS to happier living, with greater joy and potential for success. You can maintain your health in a number of ways. Total health is good health of the mind, body, and spirit.

Do activities that promote healthy living. Rid yourself of any unhealthy habits and activities that you do regularly. Be with healthy people. Spend quality time with your friends. Set aside family time. Eat what you like, but make sure that what you eat benefits your health. Some people have certain food allergies—avoid those foods. When at a restaurant or a friend's place for a meal, learn about the ingredients you are consuming so that you know with confidence what you are eating is safe for you. Go on a diet if you wish, but make sure the diet is good for *you*. Not all diets suit everyone. We are all individuals with unique bodies, sizes, and chemistries. However, everyone needs good nutrition to be healthy.

Care for more than just your physical health. Take pride in your appearance: your clothing, posture, complexion, hygiene, expressions, and mannerisms – everything that makes you a *real* person who is truly *you*. Never try to be someone you are not. Be the true you, and health will be easier to maintain. Being someone you are not is dangerous to oneself and others. Improving yourself is good, but realize there are limits to what you can do.

Sometimes, conflicts within one's own body chemistry can create a struggle with one's sexual nature. There is nothing wrong with having sexual feelings that do not conform to society's norms, as long as you feel that who you are is *right* for *you*. This will be a major contributing factor toward your health (good or bad). For those with a mental illness, knowing your true self and your personal feelings will be an important step towards healthy living. Most people with a mental illness seek to be healthy. The alternative is long-term hospitalization, institutionalization, and poor health. The above gives you something to think about. Being healthy is a choice. The time to make your choice is now.

BE ALIVE AND FEEL ALIVE

BE ALIVE, AND you will feel alive. The more you shine outwardly, the more you brighten yourself inwardly. There are a few ways to do this. Wellness training centres can be expensive and require travel to distant places. I would strongly recommend local, more affordable places. With their assistance, design a constructive goal plan.

For those who are able to self-teach, this book will provide a starting point. The finishing point depends on you, so, in a sense, there is no finishing point, but you will know inside you and in your spirit that as a person, you are a whole and well, a "finished product," largely thanks to you. Here are a few simple concepts to consider.

- To be alive and feel alive, you must apply yourself.
- Don't stay in bed.
- Don't stay in front of the TV.
- Want to be well.
- Want to be a "somebody."
- Modify your self-image by "thinking outside the box."
- Have a strong desire to change.

Outside this, nothing can stop you unless you let them. The one to worry about the most is you. The concepts are simple, but they require strength and consistency to apply them successfully. One just has to think of the difference between illness and wellness.

Look at some basic differences: How to you *look* and how do you *communicate*? Do you look lively or pale, with no expression and dull eyes? Try to display expression. This will make your eyes shine. To look less pale, spend more time out in the sun.

Another part of being alive is communication. Various forms of communication include verbal, visual, and touch. When you speak, do you sound alive? Is your appearance vibrant? Are there regular periods of contact by touch with others? When speaking, sound alive. When your voice is livelier, your face will also look more alive. To help with this, read a book of choice to yourself out loud. Try to emphasize the appropriate words with inflections. Here is a short story you can practise with. It helps if you can look into a mirror while doing this.

ONE STORMY NIGHT

ON A DARK, cool, stormy night, there were two teenage boys all alone in a big house. The rain sounded like bullets pounding down on the tin roof. Clatter and shatter could be heard outside. There was the creaking of trees and the howling wind through the valley. The river was rising with loud ripples and splashing on the dark, rough, beaten rocks along the winding shoreline.

Suddenly, there came loud clash of thunder. A brief moment later, the power in the house went out. Everything became pitch black—eerie, spooky, and frightening.

The younger brother exclaimed with fear and a slight quiver in his voice, "Brian, where are you? I'm scared."

Brian exclaimed with a reassuring voice, "Jacob, I am in Dad's favourite chair in the den with a small battery-operated lamp by my side. Can you make it in here?"

As Jacob walked down the dark hallway, he said to Brian, "I hear your voice, you are not scared, are you?"

Brian said, "When it comes to these nasty storms, I become as fearless as a lion."

As Jacob continued down the hall, the floor squeaked.

Just as Jacob saw the soft glow of the lamp by his brother, the power and house lights came on. There was also the buzzing of the water tank start-up. At the same moment came the drumming of the furnace and the whisk of warm air flowing out of the vents. Jacob was sure glad to have the lights back on so he could see the reassuring look on his brother's face.

"Sure glad to be with you," exclaimed Jacob.

All was calm. All was at peace. This event was a lot of strain. Jacob was starting to feel tired and weary. Their parents were back home. After cheerful greetings, it was time for bed. All in the house was quiet. Only the sound of the pelting rain shimmering down on the tin roof could be heard. By dawn the storm was over.

End of story.

* * *

Then there is appearance. To feel alive, one must appear alive. This will greatly promote the attraction of new friends, and new friends lead to more happiness in your life. When people like you, you like yourself all the more. When maintain a nice appearance regularly, you will want to *be* nice regularly. This affects communication on a basic level. When you appear nice, you are giving out two important messages. You are saying, "I care what you think of me" and "I care what I think of me."

Touch is a silent form of communication and can be combined with verbal communication. Here are a few simple ways to do this.

- Saying hello to someone while touching their upper arm.
- Giving someone a hug goodbye.
- Agreeing with someone (when you the situation) and saying "I know how you feel" while placing your hand on their shoulder for just a moment.
- Giving a word of sympathy with a gentle touch to the side of their upper arm.

For a formal greeting, greet a person with a hand extended to shake. If, in a brief moment, the other person does not extend their hand, then withdraw yours.

In the Western world culture, a hand shake signifies the following:

a welcome
a hello
a deal
sign of trust

THE BENEFITS OF MEDITATION

MEDITATION CAN HELP one relax and increase joy in life. Find greater peace of mind. Peace can come easier through meditation. Life comes into balance. Life responds to stress more effectively. Your mind becomes more productive and positive. You will find it easier to concentrate and make on-the-spot decisions more quickly.

For those with schizophrenia, taking the proper medication will result in clearer thoughts. The mind will stop racing. Thought processes become smoother and easier to control. There will be a potential reduction in anxiety, panic, and paranoia. There is a chance your medication will be reduced. You will gain more energy and tire less often. Stress will be reduced.

GOALS

GOAL SETTING IS important for a positive productive functional life. A goal helps direct one's life and guides one to a livelihood most suitable. Sometimes a goal does not work out how one would have hoped. Trial and error is a good method for selecting one's goals. Eventually, goals become clearer as they reveal the path of success.

For those with schizophrenia (thought process disorder), goals are definitely important. It is also important to contemplate which goals are the most obtainable, suitable, and fulfilling *for you*.

Sometimes, one will have more than one goal to accomplish in the progress of one's life. It is okay to have a number of goals. I myself have set several, and they are at various stages of completion. Some of my life goals include the following:

> social service worker diploma
> freelance writer diploma
> freelance writing
> peer support
> marriage
> teaching mental wellness

BEING RESPONSIBLE

ONE OF THE key factors in maintaining a healthy and productive lifestyle and beneficial mental wellness is to be *responsible* for ourselves. Being responsible can be difficult. In this section, I shall illustrate responsibility and non-responsibility. True-life events reflect these two principles.

In my youth, my brother and I were given the responsibility of looking after the house while our parents were going out for a few hours. In addition, we were to care for a leaky hot water tank. The leak was slow. To aid the leak required sponging up the water every eight to ten minutes. Simple, right? For our entertainment, we had the use of the TV. We also had a friend over to play games.

While entertaining ourselves, we became lazy and distracted from our responsibilities. To get around paying constant attention to the leak, we laid down layers of paper towels to absorb the water. This way, we would have more uninterrupted time to play games with our friend. We had about an hour of fun time. Our friend had to go home, so we resorted to the TV.

It was only during the TV commercials that my brother and I would attend the leak. Instead of sponging up the water, we simply laid paper towels to absorb the water. Then, when we ran out of paper towels, we resorted to using toilette tissue. Needless to say, this was a poor method to attend to the leak. But due to laziness, we shirked our responsibilities.

When our parents returned, they were more than upset for our irresponsibility. We consumed a fortune in household products. Our parents had to spend money replacing those products that my brother and I wasted. As a result, there was not enough money to take my brother and me out to dinner in return for the favour of minding the leaky hot water tank.

This illustrates that it is costlier to be lazy and irresponsible than it is to be responsible and put in an honest effort. This also illustrates the just rewards of the "play-work" ideology. As simplistic as it sounds, it applies to many situations.

LEARN FROM YOUR MISTAKES

LIVING IN THE real world, you must realize that mistakes happen. There is no way to truly undo a mistake, and you cannot "turn back the clock." You have to pick yourself up. Decide that life goes on and that you *must* go on.

A new day is always a new opportunity and fresh start. This is also true when a mistake is made. A mistake is actually a good situation. It shows you where you are in life at the moment, what was before you that moment and possible direction or change to go towards. Most people feel bad about their mistakes. That is natural and beneficial. Why is it beneficial? You learn to leave behind and move on. Just as mistakes come and go, *so does success.*

DEALING WITH THE HARD KNOCKS IN LIFE

AS MENTIONED, SOME situations, although *totally* not enjoyable, need to be dealt with in a positive, life-changing manner so that life may continue. Hard knocks in life happen to many people in all walks of life. For those with schizophrenia and other mental illnesses, hard knocks can really be devastating. However, my friend, a hard knock in life can be overcome. First you must accept that it has happened. Then you must realize that this will come to an end, even if slowly and gradually. It may even take several years to resolve.

Hard knocks in life can hang heavily in your heart and feel like an explosion, making it difficult to deal with. You can and must manage to live past it. Consider the hard knocks of life that you survive as crises from which many others would never bounce back. This makes you a stronger person.

Consider the hard knocks as the "roughness of life" helping you survive. Hard knocks hurt. Many hard knocks can never be forgotten. It also takes a strong person to stand up to the hard knocks in life. Moving forward is the only direction one can go. All other directions lead to doom, despair, and destruction.

Think about surviving in this world. You must continue to live and live life as best you can, utilizing all the resources available to you. What are a few potential resources you have available? Here are a few possible resources available in midsize and larger communities.

> community services
> counselling agencies
> credit counselling
> services for seniors
> financial institutions
> educational institutions
> medical services
> thrift stores
> public transportation
> food banks
> community meals

COPING WITH THE LOSS OF A FRIEND OR LOVED ONE

THE SUDDEN LOSS of a friend, family member, or significant other can be quite the blow to the one living through the loss—particularly the sting of just being confronted with the news.

When the sting is felt, it's natural to want to cry. It is a human response and should *not* be held back. When the news comes to a family or more than one person, people may experience a sudden drop of energy. This is because such an experience puts the body in a temporary state of shock. When this happens, one might even suffer from a fainting spell. If there two or more people are present, give each other a hug for strength, support and reassurance that everything will be okay. A hug is such a simple but effective means of crisis intervention. It shows each other the true bonding of love and care.

If a person is alone during a time of crisis, one should phone a friend or family member. Depending on circumstances, one may wish to go to a friend or neighbour's place. If one has no one to hold onto or contact, it may be of some benefit to remember the good times shared with that person.

Whether or not you are a writer, you can try writing a brief note, poem, or short letter addressed to the family member of the deceased. In that letter, write about some of the activities, particularly the times spent with each other. Include special outings and trips the two of you took together. The following is an example of this. Here is a letter I wrote for when my friend Jeff died:

> Stewart Lightstone
> Belleville, Ont.
>
> January 8, 2008
>
> To whom it may concern,
>
> I was a good friend of Jeff for many years. Here are some of my good memories of Jeff.
>
> I met Jeff a little over twenty years ago. We first met as roommates on the psychiatric ward of the Belleville General Hospital. We soon became friends. I was discharged first, but before I left, he gave me his phone number. He was discharged about a week later. I phoned him about a visit. He invited me over to his place to have dinner with

him. I forget what the meal was, but every meal I had at his place was good.

I am not sure just how we initiated the topic, but we came up with the idea for me to move into his apartment to be his boarder and eventually we would get a two-bedroom apartment. I moved in and got nicely settled in. We got along well, but Housing then informed us that I could not stay there as he was a tenant of Housing with subsidized rent. Three days after I moved in, I moved out to a furnished bachelor apartment.

I still visited him often, and we would go out to supper together about once a week and every night, on payday. It wasn't long after that before he got a transfer to Palmer Road. About a year later, I moved into the same building. Those who knew Jeff's apartment would know the layout of my apartment.

We entertained each other often with visits and meals together. One day, he introduced me to his friend Mark. The three of us would go out to restaurants and bars. One special time out was on Halloween night. Not that we dressed up in any costumes, but we each wore an unusual hat that night, and to see the three of us in a bar together, we would have made a perfect picture together. Let me also mention that when we went to a bar, it would only be the "classy" bars. It wasn't long after the three of us got together, Mark moved to Kingston.

Jeff and I went to the theatre occasionally and once attended a private New Year's Eve party in Belleville. The most exciting New Year's celebration was once we went by bus to Toronto for two nights. We stayed at a modest hotel, and on our first night there, we had a lovely dinner together. Then on the next night, New Year's Eve, we went for a short walk to a real classy hotel just around the corner from the hotel we were staying in. It turned out that at the classy hotel was a free buffet dinner with live music. We sat on very posh leather chairs and enjoyed one strong drink each. After a while there, we decided to go back to our hotel to see the New Year in.

We returned to Belleville later on New Year's Day. For all the time I knew Jeff, he seldom had a strong drink, loved dining, and regularly went out for coffee with me. We would celebrate our Birthdays together because our birthdays where only two days apart Jeff was a good friend and a good person and shall be missed.

Sincerely,
Stewart Lightstone

PRODUCTIVE AND LEISURE TIME

PRODUCTIVE TIME BY oneself is important. Leisure time for oneself is also important. A balanced life of productive time and leisure time is part of one's healthy wellbeing.

To determine the balance between leisure time and productive time, one must learn the meaning of leisure time and productive time. One must first learn what they intend to accomplish during both leisure and productive time. What life goals do you have? What dreams do you wish to see come true?

Leisure is an activity not requiring a work-related routine or stressful situation. A leisurely activity may be physical and even physically exhausting but should be entertaining and fun to do for the individual.

A productive activity is one that involves some form of work. The work performed produces a tangible end result of something that was gained by the act of productivity.

Having known the meaning of leisure and, one can now have a clearer understanding of *what* they intend to accomplish and *how much* they intend to accomplish for both productive time and leisure time. By measuring one's current leisure time and the amount of leisure time desired, one better understands how to adjust their productive time. With this in mind, one of three outcomes may be realized.

It may well turn out that productive time and leisure time are sitting at the desired balance. It may be that productive time is currently too inflated for one's desired lifestyle or one's time is too inflated.

To clearly know the balance of leisure or productive time mentioned above, one should make a list of what occupies their day, week, and month. This list may help jar your memory.

Sleep, bath, mealtime, shower, writing, dressing, walking, bussing, driving, office work, factory work, car maintenance, shopping, coffee break, singing, playing a musical instrument, worship your Devine one, attending house of worship, reading, watching TV, celebrating a special day or event, house renovations, house repairs, self-defence, learning self-defence, cooking, raking the leaves, lawn mowing, lawn bowling, travelling across the city, town, country, or ocean, camping, swimming, sorting out the house/office files, taking out the garbage, recycling, composting, trip to the vet, going to your doctor/dentist, gardening/weeding, watering the lawn, picking flowers, having a walk through a park, washing windows, delivering the newspaper/mail, opening gifts/boxes and letters, working at a hobby, baking, answering the phone/door/answering machine, listening to music, playing card games/computer games/ board games, typing, keeping up your hygiene, washing dishes, doing the laundry, putting together a puzzle, vacuuming, sweeping, mopping, artwork, crafts, reading the newspaper, checking the mail, banking, buying lottery tickets, making the bed, taking daily vitamins/medication, relaxing, taking an afternoon nap, feeding/caring for and playing with your pet, schoolwork, college work, going to the theatre, dining out, dancing, listening to the rustle of the trees, walking the dog, shovelling the snow.

I think by now you have the idea. Now to write out your own list.

THE IMPORTANCE OF FAMILY AND FRIENDS

EVERYONE NEEDS PEER support. Your primary peer support is your family members, followed by your friends (in that order of importance).

The family unit, since the mid-1980s has taken on many forms. There was the family of four (father, mother, son, and daughter). Then came the "nuclear family" of father, mother, and one child. In 1985, the typical family was, for a short while, father, mother, and 1.5 children. After this came the extended nuclear family—father, mother, child, and one or two adopted children. By this time, we were also seeing families of mixed cultures and different faiths. Some of these families would honour only one of the faiths in the family. Some families would observe the multitude of faiths. I myself grew up with a father and mother of different faiths. We, to some extent, observed both faiths. My brother married into a different culture. He will soon celebrate his eleventh anniversary, and he and his wife are doing quite well together. Also in the family, there have been three other unions of mixed background. Despite the strong mixture of cultures in the family, there have been strong relationships. This sort of scenario has been continuing throughout Canada and the United

States. In Europe, Europeans have stayed strong in maintaining their own unique culture.

As world populations continue to increase, there has been a stronger push for small families and some married couples not to have children. As families incline to have only one child, that child receives more attention from their parents. The parents face differences too. They might have grown up with brothers and/or sisters. Since twenty-five to thirty-five years ago, there have been many families with two or more children. Naturally, these children had more peers to grow into and become friends with.

Now it has become more important for spouses to rely on each other. Children have to rely on fewer but closer friends. With smaller family ties and smaller circles of close friends, mutual support has become all the more important. Therefore, it has become more important to rely on each other.

With family and friends being increasingly of mixed cultures, such integration has required coexisting and cooperating with each other. Now more than ever in human history, we need to rely on each other. This requires communication, sharing of technology and natural resources, healthcare, education, safety, and the welfare of all people. These are a just a few reasons why it is important for family and friends to interact with each other as best we can.

Some families with many members can be considered a clan. Within the clan, there are family financial advisors, the well-educated who provide new ideas and innovate the clan to ensure progress and thus the clan's survival. There are elders for wisdom, and the children all trained to one day be the clan's future leaders. A family clan has its dangers as well. Some members of the clan may not do as well as others. Some may have a mental illness or other disability. Those with a disability will likely never be the head of the clan, even if they are the eldest child. They will probably have a say in important family decisions but never the one in control. With my own experience, I share control with my brother. I always have an equal stance and equal vote. This is important for a functional family that stands on a firm family foundation.

Some people with a disability on a disability plan/pension among their family are sometimes taken advantage of by their family. In one such case, a person placed their sister in charge of their finances. This person even had their sister purchase and deliver the groceries to their apartment. The groceries were not always suitable. There would be continual spoilage with some of the groceries because some items were over stocked while some essential groceries were understocked. Shamefully, this person's family, when taking them out to dinner, would *never* take them out to any real "fine" dining. In short, this is a clear example of a "dysfunctional" family with a bad family foundation.

Friends can be like a secondary family. I myself have one friend who my mother would sometimes refers to as her "third son" (having only two sons by birth).

Friends are beneficial for the absence of family. Friends often help family situations that need an outside party. Friends can help in time of need or crisis. Family will likely help too for these needs, but it is always wise to have additional support. These days of crisis situations could cost thousands of dollars. Few people have multiple thousands of dollars on hand to hand out. Therefore, having all the extra financial support is wise, practical, and realistic, particularly with close friends whom one can ask for support to make the difference between "disaster" and "just fine."

When children are old enough to go to school, they begin to leave family and meet friends. From this point on, they begin learning by teachers—*real* impact teaching from their friends. Friends influence us greatly. We often fashion our image, our clothing style, our likes and dislikes, and our first-time experiences with love and hate. We also discover ourselves with what we are on the inside. Our values grow and change as we live and interact with our friends.

Friends (in adult years) are often more available than family. This is because you will likely be around friends more than family will. Family is important. Family in one's early years teach us many important basic life skills. As young folk and toddlers, we learn language, writing, speaking, and acceptable behaviour.

Those with schizophrenia and other mental illnesses are eventually admitted into hospital. When admitted into hospital for psychiatric care, the first time, the first thing they need is rest. The next part of treatment is medication (trial tests) and then a support team. The components of a support team could be a psychiatrist, nurse or family doctor, family, and friends (particularly close friends).

As part of the recovery process, once the patient is getting close to stable, they need the introduction of their support team. It is cautioned not to have the person "bombarded" with people. Someone in recovery needs periods of days, weeks, or months by themselves. This period is to sort out their thoughts.

Then the person in recovery should spend regular daily time with friends and close friends. The above may differ slightly, depending on the nature of the person.

LIVING "OUTSIDE THE BOX"

FOR OPTIMUM, PREFERRED living, to be your greatest potential, one *must* live and think outside the box. What is the "box"? What is "outside"? Is there an "inside" the box? How can this work for someone with a disability?

The "box" is one's normal, comfortable standard of life that seems secure to them. To go "outside" the box is to venture *away* from comfort and security to achieve one's fullest potential. Staying "inside" the box may *stunt* the development and quality of the life you could have. Life inside the box is like staying in a comfortable chair and staying there without any desirable future. This is because if you stay in that comfortable chair (so to say), you get nowhere in life. In time, the chair gets old and loses its comfort, and then you end up with a dull, dreary life.

Living outside the box can work easily for someone living with a disability. A slow and gradual build-up with real results can be accomplished. The first step is to have determination. Then, you must live outside the box to lead a more fulfilling life than what you already have. Next, you have to know what is holding you inside the box, and then you have to tear it down. Initially, you can do this by concentrated thought within your mind. Know your mind, and you will know your weaknesses and strengths. Improve your weaknesses as best you can; build up your strengths at the same time.

Seek some of your desires and go for them. Eventually, with constant progress and effort, you will reach the outer barriers of "your box." Then, be determined to push beyond the barriers of the box. You are then finally outside the box. It may be hard at first, and it may take time, but never give up.

YOU ARE WHAT YOU DO AND WHAT YOU THINK

WHY DO YOU think the way you do? Are you happy that way? Is your health a reflection on how you think? These are important questions to think about. This part of the book (all by its own) can totally change your life for the rest of your life the way you think affects all aspects of your life. This is a lifelong endeavour to develop your life to its fullest.

What all is determined by what and how you think? There are a number of aspects that determine how you think and will affect you and your life. To name a few:

> the way you talk
> the way you look at life and the world around you
> your mannerisms

your daily conduct
your degree of wealth (or degree of poverty)
your appearance
your education and your degree of happiness (or depression)

There is more, but what is listed above can really change your life. Most important, the way you think will greatly contribute to the success of controlling schizophrenia.

Let me tell you something very important: never think in black and white (unless you're an accountant). Life is usually in constant shades of grey. The law is supposed to be black and white, but sometimes it is not.

Some wholesome ways of thinking could be as follows. Instead of Have watching TV, read the daily paper. Instead of skipping school, become the best student. Instead of sleeping more than ten hours a night, try to get up after eight. Make sure never to sleep the day away.

Many people with schizophrenia and other mental illnesses want to feel useful but are unable to hold down a job for a month. A various list of volunteer work is needed in most communities. Try to get a volunteer job for a day or more a week. Volunteer for short hours, and gradually increase the hours and frequency. I know from firsthand experience (even with volunteer work), down the road, *reward will come.*

Some people with a disability are held back in life because of limited living skills or lack of experience. This need not be so. If you are a poor housekeeper, try to be a "moderate" housekeeper by doing a few easy tasks, and *don't* stress yourself out for not doing everything.

BUILDING CONFIDENCE

TO CONTROL SCHIZOPHRENIA and other mental illnesses, one must have confidence. You build confidence in layers. You need the first layer to be your foundation. The foundation is made by you knowing yourself and knowing the real self. To know your real self, you must part from any falsehood of yourself and eliminate anything that might be phoney or a false front. You do that by knowing where you are right now, where you have been the past year, and where you will likely be a year from now. What is phoney (of that period) is whatever you found to be uncomfortable or you dislike about yourself. When you find the real "you" that you are firmly comfortable with, then you will know what "you" is. This is the first layer of confidence.

The second layer of confidence is what you thirst for and the knowledge that you have the ability to get it. Completely break down all the parts of what you want in life, study it, and learn the most you can about what you want most. Know and be firm with what you want for your life the next ten years. This is a very important step in the journey of your life. As you take this journey, you build the confidence you need to complete your journey with the best success rate you can achieve. You now have the thickest layer of confidence.

The final layer of confidence is also the hardest to build and maintain. Gradually, this layer will become the strongest layer of your confidence, almost as thick as the second layer.

You eventually learn what drives you forward in life. You will learn your quest in life. You must feel your quest in your heart. Open your heart to receive and capture your quest. This is the desire to pull your life in the direction to become filled with the joy of your quest. This feeling will accelerate and is the taste of confidence that binds you to who you really are. With good health and wellbeing of your mind, your confidence will be at its peak.

Sound mind and success in life will become your ultimate reward in life. This is the height of confidence. Maintaining your confidence is the natural process of life. To live life how it feels right for you is the key for forming everlasting confidence. My friend, the world is now yours.

SOCIALIZING

FOR FURTHER CONTROL of schizophrenia, it is extremely important to socialize. One cannot take control schizophrenia being by oneself. Now, it's true—it is important to take time to be by oneself, including the occasional solitude. At times, during the battle with schizophrenia, one may need to be in hospital.

Humans are social by nature. Throughout history, to this day, we have needed to be with other people simply to survive as a species. Without socializing with others, we would not be well. However, many with schizophrenia find it difficult to socialize. I will now provide a few ideas about socializing, but following up on this is up to you. A word of caution: do *not* use the personal ads or online dating sites. What is important is to be *with* people. There may be singles dances in your community. That would be good to consider, but it is not a long-term solution.

Places of education, gathering places, and hobby groups are ideal. Being with your peer age groups is a standard, but people within a range of ten years or more may gather, and this is okay.

How does one find likeminded people? At the public library, there are often bulletin boards that advertise community events of *various* interests. The cost of these are usually low, perhaps even free. Can you afford $5.00 and a brown-bagged lunch?

Take a stroll in the downtown core of your community. You will see many posters in restaurant windows. You will find a variety of entertainment, activities, out-of-town day trips, and many other social activities.

IN CLOSING

THIS BOOK HAS been written thanks to family, friends, wisdom, knowledge, and many references to my own firsthand experiences. In closing, I would like to thank you for taking the time *and effort* to read this book. *Now,* I strongly command you: Don't be me. *Be you!*

APPENDIX A: GUIDANCE FOR CAREGIVERS

Caregivers often overlook what the person with schizophrenia had going for themselves before they became ill. Do you know some of the careers that came shattering down because of their illness? Some of those I have met were previously doctors, nurses, ministers (of a church), social workers, teachers, counsellors, musicians, officers in the military, electronic technicians, and office administrators. What became of them? They would spend years in psychiatric institutions. When finally discharged from hospital, they would be put on a low fixed income. They would spend hours in a coffee shop having a coffee and a cigarette. Some would be starving artists, painting their hopes on canvas that often would sell without profit, perhaps sold for a pack of cigarettes. Some worked delivering packages or pizzas, filling in for a part-time job, working as a crossing guard, delivering newspapers, mowing lawns, and often volunteering, paid with bus tickets and free coffees. Do you now see a significant contrast between before and after?

Your loved ones have been through a lot. They have gone through psychosis and time in hospital, tried on different medications and dosages, with various side effects. They have dealt with pain and discomfort and disrupted sleeping patterns, have had their friends treat them differently just because of the changes and actions of the ill person. These people need time for rest and rebound.

You will have to change too. You will need to be a good communicator and a good listener. You will need to gain knowledge and advice to assist the person manage their treatment and manage their life.

Although some actions may need tolerance, some actions should *never* be tolerated in order for the person to make the right choices, learn from their mistakes, and pay the just penalties for their actions.

The person has rights, and their rights must be given as allowed by law. The government has certain control. The doctors and hospitals have certain control. The person under treatment should be treated as an equal within the family unit and in society at large.

Caregivers also have the role of "advocate." There may come a time when one has to speak or act on someone's behalf to have the greatest benefit for the person. There may be legal issues to deal with. This would-be additional responsibilities for caregivers.

Caregivers also have the responsibility to care for themselves to caregivers need time for themselves with time to sleep and eat. There is the need to manage their own health in good state.

APPENDIX B: WHAT THINGS CAN I DO?

I have schizophrenia.
I can manage my own apartment.
I can do the chores responsible in an apartment.
Laundry, scrub floors, iron, vacuum, dishes, sweep, wash windows.
I can handle my own bank account.
I can love and be loved.
I can learn, I can cook, I can write, and I can think.
I can choose and follow a faith.
I can have a significant relationship.
I can be married. I can be a parent.
I can be a grandparent. I can be an uncle or aunt.
I can shop for food. I can shop for clothing.
I can look after a pet.
I can use a computer. I can "surf the net."
I can play games, indoor or outdoor.
I can choose the decor my house/apartment.
I can celebrate my birthday.
I can celebrate other significant events.
I can attend parties and other socials.
I can drive a car.
I can participate and contribute to "pot-luck" dinners.
I can go out dancing or to night clubs.
I can graduate from school, college, or university.

I can have a job or have a career.
I can write a book to help others.
I can go on a camping trip.
I can participate in community events.
I can be an active part of the community.
I can control a diet, lose weight, or gain weight.
I can be a member of a fitness club.
I can travel, by car, bus, train, plane, or boat.
I can entertain guests.
I can enter tournaments.
I can do the Terry Fox Run.
I can be an advocate for a cause dear to heart.
I can feel emotions (emotionally well, emotionally hurt) and mend emotional pain.
I can accept people, and people can accept me.
I can know my state of mental wellbeing and know when I need help.
I can experience success. I can celebrate my success.
I can experience failure and rebound from it.
I can hope and I can do what means important to me.
Above all, *I can control schizophrenia.*

APPENDIX C: LIST OF PLACES I TRAVELLED TO FOR RESEARCH

to Write This Book

- Toronto
- Oshawa
- Trenton
- Picton
- Ottawa
- Nepean
- Kingston
- Brockville
- Belleville

APPENDIX D: THE DIFFERENCE BETWEEN A SICK PERSON AND A WELL PERSON

It is pursued by most people to be a well person. To tell the difference between a sick person and a well person is to first describe a sick person and then describe a well person.

A sick person may not actually appear sick. It is what you can tell from inside the mind and the person's habits, actions and daily activities that you can tell the person is sick. What are some of these signs? The mind of a sick person is full of negatives—negative thoughts, negative desires, negative attitudes, negative attractions, and most of all, a negative view of themselves.

These people are often sad and depressed. Their ego is low. Their appearance may be dirty or not well kept. They create a negative living environment that reinforces their negative state of living.

The way they perceive themselves, the people, peers, and the world around them are usually very negative. Sometimes so negative that they can be considered mentally sick and often sicken the people they are around daily. They quite often have a lifestyle that is unhealthy and destructive. This destructive cycle may also carry on to those they spend the day with. These people have a high risk of being in either a psychiatric facility or corrections institution.

This can be changed. They can become well, positive person with intense applied consistent effort. First, they need to know what a well person is and how a well person conducts themselves, their life, and their lifestyle.

WHAT IS A WELL PERSON?

A WELL PERSON can be almost anyone. An ill person can be almost anyone. What is the main difference? Any person (including an ill person) who *wants* to become a well person is the main difference. Once well, even if still taking medication, it is a lot easier to maintain wellness than to transform from ill to well.

What are some of the characteristics of a well person? How does an ill person become a well person? Let's discuss these two points.

A well person thinks of themselves as a positive person and sees the community and the world in a positive perspective. They see their peers as positive people, and those peers *not* positive minded are gotten rid of. A well person avoids problems. When a well person has a problem, he or she deals with it quick and swiftly and will always have a solution, even if the solution is not desirable or takes time to apply.

A well person continually works on maintaining a real sense of wellness mentally, physically, spiritually, socially, and emotionally. They have goals in life they know they can obtain. They have an ultimate goal with a sensible and well formulated plan to achieve the goal.

A well person takes good care of their body, mind, and appearance. A well person helps themselves first and others second. A well person takes control of their lives. Some of the aspects of taking control of your life are responsibility or your actions. These include but are not limited to the following:

> diet
> daily activities

home and home environment
finances
plans for their future

A well person uses all their skills, further develops their skills, and learns the skills they may need to continue their goals, wishes, and wants in the future.

A well person rarely worries about their life, but any worries that do come are overcome and as quickly as possible. A well person sees ahead of time of any illness that may come to be and seeks help so that any potential illness is "nipped in the bud."

How does an ill person become well? An ill person studies all the characteristics of a well person. How does a person obtain the characteristics of a well person? If a person is capable of learning, then by observing well people and the lifestyle of well people, one day at a time, they themselves, with application, will become well. The degree of learning is not a high level of learning at all. An average third-grade student would have the minimum level of learning required.

However, if a person on their way to wellness ever give up or stopped pursuing wellness, they could easily backslide to being an ill person. Also, if taking medication, do not stop doing so unless directed by your doctor. Stopping your medication can really stop your progression to wellness and possibly stop you from living a worthwhile life. It can even lead to death. This nobody should want. Where there is life, there is hope. Where there is no life, there is *no* hope.

APPENDIX E: HAVING A PET

First, it is not recommended to have an exotic animal as a pet. Second, fish may look nice, but they provide very little amusement and are difficult to keep healthy for long periods. As for bird (of any type), they are usually pretty. Most of the time, they need to be caged, but they are meant to fly and should be allowed to do so (provided it is safe to have the bird fly around *without escaping*). Having a bird flying around presents the risk of the bird getting into someone's hair, or the bird could leave a mess on the furniture—or, even worse, on a visiting person.

There are advantages to having a pet. A pet can be great therapy for someone with a mental illness such as schizophrenia. A pet can be a friend. A pet can provide company, even when curled up on the couch. There is a living animal in your midst. There is a living being, in a sense. If your pet is a cat or dog, these animals think. They have intelligence and an awareness of you and those who come over to visit.

A pet is dependent on you. They need your assistance to feed them, provide water to drink, and a place in your home that they quickly know to come back to when outdoors for a while. They need you to clean out their litter box or take them out for a walk. There are health needs of a pet. There include annual shots and medication for various health needs, as people have. For some dogs, there is the need for shelter for long-term stay outdoors. There is strong need for pet population control. This requires the pets to be spayed or neutered. Then, at the end of the pet's life (as for all of us), comes death. This can occur naturally in their sleep, when they are hit by a car, when they are attacked by another animal, or if the need comes to "put down" the pet at a vet or animal shelter. This is always hard, no matter what the cause of death is.

The final consideration is cost. There are monthly costs and annual costs.

This works out to be about 7 percent of your income. I lived this out in *real life* for eleven years with the cat I used to have.

APPENDIX F: "YOU CAN BE HAPPY"

You can be happy. Just turn around,
Look at yourself and see you as you are.
Go ahead. If a happy person you want to see,
You will see a happy person.
Tell yourself in the mirror and say, "I can be happy."
If you are not happy,
Learn from those who are happy.
You can be happy.
Go be with happy people and see happy people.
To know happiness and whom are happy people.
You can be happy.
You can be happy.
If I can be happy, you can be happy too.
Make the world a little happier
By yourself being happy.
When you see happy people, it will help you to be happy.
If you want to be happy, *decide* to be happy.
You will.

APPENDIX G: POSITIVE REINFORCEMENTS FOR SELF-USE

- Attractive
- Brave
- Careful
- Caring
- Charismatic
- Charitable
- Charming
- Colourful
- Commendable
- Compassionate
- Considerate
- Courageous
- Creative
- Energetic
- Faithful
- Friendly
- Generous
- Gifted
- Good Inner Karma
- Happy
- Healthy
- Helpful
- Honourable
- Honourable
- Hopeful
- Humane
- Humble
- Impressible
- Impressive
- Ingenious
- *Ingenuity*
- Interesting
- Joyful
- Kind
- Likeable
- Logical
- Lovable
- Noble
- Outgoing
- Peaceful
- Personable/Talkative
- Positive

- Protective
- Reliable
- Respectable
- Respectful
- Sensible
- Sensitive
- Smart
- Sociable
- Spiritual
- Supportive/Empathetic
- Talented
- Tasteful
- Thankful
- Thoughtful
- Trustful
- Trustworthy
- Useful
- Wise
- Wonderful

APPENDIX H: YOUR "HELP LINE PHONE LIST"

"Top 3"

Community Services Hot Line	613-555-1212
Brian (friend)	613-555-3121
Florence (neighbour)	613-555-0977

Family

Brother	613-555-7433
Sister	613-555-5643
Father	613-555-0988
Mother	613-555-0988
Aunt	418-555-5542
Uncle	418-555-1174
Cousin	419-555-6754
In-law	418-555-0978

APPENDIX I: GLOSSARY OF TERMS AND DEFINITIONS

Words often associated with the lives of psychiatrics/survivors (not alphabetical).

Schizophrenia. Misfired, disrupted, or fragmented electrical signals going through the brain cells. This will lead to many observed effects, including the following: (1) false perceptions of your senses, particularly audio and visual; (2) delusional thoughts, including thoughts of grandeur.

Thought process disorder. When one's thoughts are frequently out of order.

Thoughts of grandeur. Thoughts and beliefs of self as unreal and/or being an extraordinary entity or being that is far greater than the common person, possibly with special powers that only self-possess.

Delusions. Thoughts that are not real but are real to self.

Consumer/survivor. A person who has spent time on a psychiatric ward or psychiatric hospital that has gone on antipsychotic medication, has consumed mental health services, and is managing well with their treatment.

Caregiver. A person (usually a spouse or family member) who cares for a psychiatric survivor or ill person.

Superficial. Something not real but real to you.

Bombarded. Something repeatedly hitting the same target more than necessary.

Recovery. Stages from illness to wellness.

Shock treatment. Electrical shocks to the brain destroying brain cells causing permanent and irreversible damage to the brain.

Antipsychotics. Medication designed to treat psychotic conditions of a mental illness.

Bubble of hope. A small world where all your hopes and dreams live for a while and suddenly breaks apart and is gone.

Outside partner. (1) A supportive individual who may or may not be a friend that helps one that needs a little extra help than what a caregiver can provide.

(2) One could be considered to be an assistant to the caregiver. (3) One could be considered to be someone outside the situation looking in (that could be of help).

Rock bottom. The worst one can be in one's frame of mind, through their entire history of mental illness.

Psychiatric survivor. Someone who has been admitted into a hospital psychiatric ward or psychiatric hospital with a stay of more than twenty-four hours, diagnosed with a mental illness, is discharged and managing life well enough not to be in an institution.

Alcohol. Liquid poison.

Communication. The process of giving another person an idea or concept from your mind to theirs.

Perfection. Something or someone without any error or malfunction or flaw (never found in the *real* world).

Obsession. Overly involved with someone or something to a point where you are imprisoned in your own little world, which consists mainly of the subject of the obsession.

Mentally stable. A state of mind in which one is still afflicted by the illness but well enough to function in society, possibly able for employment, and at least able to care for themselves independently. This may also be the requirement for psychiatric discharge.

Write-off. Someone beyond treatment and forever dependent for a caregiver or doctor to keep living, who will *never* achieve mental wellness or stability. Quite likely, someone who is a write off will be in a mental institution for life. (This is what I thought I was when first time hospitalized.)

Medication. A solid or injected substance containing chemicals combined with natural ingredients to cause a mind-altering affect; potentially lethal regardless of dosage.

A substance intended to help a life that may otherwise destroy a life, themselves, or another person. In general, a psychotic stabilizer.

Printed in the United States
by Baker & Taylor Publisher Services